The "Tragic Mulatta" Revisited

RACE AND NATIONALISM IN NINETEENTH-CENTURY ANTISLAVERY FICTION

EVE ALLEGRA RAIMON

RUTGERS UNIVERSITY PRESS

New Brunswick, New Jersey, and London

Library of Congress Cataloging-in-Publication Data

Raimon, Eve Allegra, 1957–
      The "tragic mulatta" revisited : race and nationalism in nineteenth-century antislavery fiction / Eve Allegra Raimon.
         p.   cm.
      Includes bibliographical references (p.) and index.
      ISBN 0-8135-3481-X (alk. paper) — ISBN 0-8135-3482-8 (pbk. : alk. paper)
         1. American fiction—19th century—History and criticism. 2. Race in literature.   3. Nationalism and literature—United States—History—19th century.   4. African American women in literature.   5. Antislavery movements in literature.   6. Racially mixed people in literature.   7. Tragic, The, in literature. 8. Nationalism in literature.   9. Slavery in literature.   10. Women in literature.   I. Title.
      PS374.R32R35   2004
      813'.3093522—dc22
                                                                          2004000308
      British Cataloging-in-Publication data for this book is available from the British Library.

Copyright © 2004 by Eve Raimon

Manufactured in the United States of America

For Mary V. Dougherty

The "Tragic Mulatta"
Revisited

CONTENTS

Acknowledgments

It is a commonplace in the genre of acknowledgments to write that one's book could not have been completed without the help of many colleagues and friends, and I am not about to transgress that generic expectation here–especially since it's the truth. To begin at the beginning, then, the foundational and invaluable scholarship of Carolyn L. Karcher provided the initial inspiration for my topic. In its early stages, I received vital encouragement from Phillip Brian Harper, who remains a model for me in both his scholarship and his pedagogy. John Burt and Michael T. Gilmore also helped shape the project. Jean Fagan Yellin offered constructive commentary on a portion of the manuscript titled "Numbering by Colors: Anti-Slavery Fiction and the 'New' Census of 1850," delivered to the 2000 American Studies Association convention. Michael Bennett's comments were most useful in sharpening the focus and the language of this study. For guiding this book into publication, I thank Leslie Mitchner and the staff of Rutgers University Press, especially Molly Baab and Melanie Halkias. Robert Burchfield deserves thanks, too, for his careful copyediting.

Deep appreciation goes to Lisa Botshon, Laura Browder, Monica Chiu, Robin Hackett, Rebecca Herzig, Melinda Plastas, and Siobhan Senier, who read and critiqued most or all of the book's chapters. They are chiefly responsible for keeping this undertaking under sail and on course. A special thanks to Timothy Powell for opening the right doors. Lisa MacFarlane and Andrea Newlyn provided generous feedback and help at key points along the way.

The University of Southern Maine (USM), Lewiston-Auburn College furnished much needed research support. It has been a congenial and rewarding place to work, and for that I'd like to thank all of my colleagues. I owe a special debt of gratitude to Rose Cleary, David Harris, Jan Hitchcock, Betty Robinson, and Robert Schaible. I have had the distinct pleasure of working with some very talented students as well, including Monique Bartlett, Syd Danforth, Iris Guillemette, Dana Lowell, Gail Monahan, Michelle Morgan, and Penny Sargent. USM librarian Evelyn Greenlaw deserves particular mention for her zeal in attaining necessary material. My colleagues in the Women's Studies Program at USM also warrant recognition for their dedication and commitment to intellectual rigor.

These acknowledgments would be incomplete without recognizing the unflagging support of such friends as Regina Pistilli and Ellen Seeling, who nourished me in ways beyond measure. Thanks also to Deborah Shields for her keen eye and her discerning ear.

I am also grateful to my sister, Martha Raimon, for her forbearance, and to my late parents, Eunice and Robert Raimon, who pointed me in the direction of academic life without ever trying.

Finally, I wish to acknowledge Mary V. Dougherty, who assisted me with the latter stages of the manuscript and whose love and luminescence seem to make all things possible.

*The "Tragic Mulatta"
Revisited*

Introduction

THE CLOSING YEARS of the twentieth century and the early years of the twenty-first have witnessed a renewal and rearticulation of the United States's long-standing fascination with interracialism.[1] Nowhere was this preoccupation with cross-racialism more evident than in the 2000 census. Politicians and census board officials wrangled over how best to quantify racial intermixture, finally inviting respondents to check multiple boxes indicating their "mixed" racial status.[2] Yet this is not the first time the construction of the U.S. census has signaled a watershed moment in the nation's long struggle to delineate racial boundaries. The mid-nineteenth century was another such dynamic period in census taking, when notions of blackness based on "one drop" of African ancestry were in formation. Signal reforms were made to the 1850 survey that suggest an earlier instance of an ongoing struggle over the construction of racial difference and its interconnectedness with American identity. That year, for the first time in U.S. history, the individual rather than the household was made the primary unit of analysis. This single innovation transformed the count from a simple apportionment tool to a complex system of data gathering in which race—among other characteristics—was newly classified and enumerated. Whereas 1840 census takers counted only groupings of whites, free persons of color, and slaves, the 1850 schedule posed detailed questions about individual slaves and, for the first time, their "colour." As it happens, these reforms were proposed at exactly the same time as the Compromise of 1850 was being debated in Congress, provoking heated sectional disputes over the purpose of the new schedule.[3] Were the new questions meant to track the increasing "blending" of America, as Northerners contended, or, as Southerners suspected, were they intended to expose the sexually corrupt underside of Southern plantation life? In fact, the first versions of the new form contained questions about the number of children born to female slaves, as well as questions about slaves' "degree of removal from pure white and black races," but the Senate acceded to proslavery demands and removed these items from the final version.[4] By devising this new, broader system of racial classification, the Thirty-first Congress in 1850 responded to political pressures associated with a rapidly changing racial demographic in much the same way as Congress did for the 2000 census. In both eras, government acknowledged the persistent fact of racial intermixture and the complexities of American identity by reconfiguring its system of racial demarcation—and in both eras, the political implications for "who counted" were profound with respect to national as much as racial self-definition.

Indeed, the 1850s marked the precise moment of U.S. racial and national identity formation when the status of American nationalism and the nation's racial composition were at once in crisis. Judicial, statutory, social, and scientific debates about the meaning of racial difference coincided with disputes over frontier expansion, which were never merely about land acquisition but also literally about what complexion the frontier would take on. Illustratively, one Northern Free-Soiler expressed a common sentiment when he exclaimed about President James K. Polk's efforts to annex Cuba that the United States did not want a territory that was filled with "black, mixed, degraded, and ignorant, or inferior races." Northerners opposed extending slavery to Cuba, but neither did many want to see a growing and supposedly inassimilable population of free Cuban citizens as part of the American republic.[5] In this way, abolitionist sentiment coexisted uneasily with rhetorics of racialism and expansionism.

The moment of midcentury marks the ascendance of Anglo-Saxon idolatry and the threat of contamination by black "blood," as well as the emergence of scientific racism and its theories of black inferiority based on polygenesis and the fields of phrenology and physiognomy. Elise Lemire has shown that such biologizing of racial difference in the period served the function of policing racial categories and enforcing white supremacy without seeming racist or opposing the ideals of a liberal democracy.[6] Thus, an early-nineteenth-century attitude of qualified acceptance with respect to interracial unions—especially in the lower South—gave way to one of growing hostility at midcentury, due in part to increasing demand for slave labor in the new territories. According to Joel Williamson, "Slavery in the 1850s needed slaves for its westward movement, and it was almost as if it possessed an intelligence that deliberately decided that it would takes slaves wherever it could get them—even if those slaves were nearly white."[7] That congruence of racialism and expansionism helped shape antebellum public policy, most famously in the Fugitive Slave Act of 1850. As Scott L. Malcolmson has pointed out, the law in effect "made every free black person a potential slave."[8] Thus, the convergent discourses of nationalist ideology, scientific racialism, and manifest destiny were at once enjoying widespread legitimacy and worked in concert as frameworks for considering matters of land, sectionalism, and national and racial character. In this way, they acted to cement political systems and structures of power that at once helped to secure—and imperil—the Union.

Concurrently, the antebellum years witnessed the evolution in the North of an aggressive nationalist ideology from which the South was excluded. In her analysis of this brand of "northern nationalism," Mary Grant argues that the national consensus that had emerged from the revolutionary era had collapsed: "North and South held increasingly disparate views of America's purpose and destiny, and by the 1850s, there was no truly national sense of the American nation."[9] Eva Saks has mapped this sense of a fragmented and fractious body politic onto the mixed-race body from a juridical standpoint. To her, "[t]he jurisprudence of miscegenation was the site for working out political issues of Federalism and race, and the human body the fractured medium of this struggle."[10] Of course, the term *miscegenation* itself has an interesting and troubling history. Its first documented use was not until 1863 in an anonymous pamphlet entitled "Miscegenation: The Theory of the Blending of the Races, Applied to the American White Man and Negro." Purporting to be written from the point of view of a radical Republican championing the cause of racial intermixing, the publication was, in fact, a cynical attempt by Democrats to scandalize Northern white voters with the prospect of widespread "amalgamation."[11]

If the courtroom offers one venue for the representational eruption of these vexed and interlocking issues, the contentious figure of the "tragic mulatto" provides a central literary site for black and white antislavery writers to work through questions raised by the highly charged subject position of mixed-race persons in antebellum society. Literally embodying both Northern and Southern ideologies, the "amalgamated" mulatto (to use the contemporaneous term) can be viewed as quintessentially American, a precursor to contemporary motifs of "hybrid" and "mestizo" identities. Hugely popular and politically influential at midcentury, the trope operates as a vehicle for exploring the complexities surrounding the interrelated identifications of race and national allegiance. For abolitionist writers of both races, the "tragic mulatto" allows for considerations of such important questions as whether mixed-race slaves can achieve freedom and independence, whether they can become integrated into the larger culture, and whether their children can prosper in the increasingly precarious Union. More fundamentally still, it functions as a device to investigate what place mixed-race persons are going to occupy in the new republic and indeed whether the Union itself can survive such profound divisions over race.

Of course, the very phrase "tragic mulatto" has a fraught history and status in literary studies, its genealogy dating back at least to Sterling Brown's *The Negro in American Fiction* (1937). Because of the " 'single drop of midnight in her veins,' " Brown maintains, the mixed-race figure must "go down to a tragic end."[12] In her groundbreaking 1978 study, *Neither White Nor Black: The Mulatto Character in American Fiction*, Judith Berzon portrays the literary device as "an outcast, a wanderer, one alone. He is the fictional symbol of marginality."[13] As evidenced by her use of the masculine pronoun in the preceding quotation, Berzon, Sterling, and many later critics focus on issues relevant to the trope's gender without really questioning its masculinist appellation. By contrast, I hope to trouble both the substance and the form of these critiques by exploring the intersection of the emblem's gendered subject position within the contingencies of national identity. Though Berzon employs the masculine form of the noun in referring to the emblem, as is typical, the fact is that it is a misnomer. Rather, it is imperative to the narrative aims of this body of literature for the "tragic mulatt*o*" to be a "tragic mulatt*a*." The very tragedy of the figure's fate depends upon her female gender. The sexual vulnerability of a female light-skinned slave is essential to propel the plot forward and to generate the reader's sympathy and outrage. Hence, the burgeoning of the genre of sentimental fiction in the early decades of the nineteenth century coincided with the appearance of the refined, orphaned, mixed-race slave character whose "tragic" destiny is overdetermined by the iniquities of plantation slavery. Predictably, if ironically, then, even as the "white blood" coursing through the veins of a male light-skinned bondman afforded him greater intelligence and subjectivity in period literature, his female counterpart was deployed simultaneously to demonstrate the destructive potential of the slave system to such a heroine's very survival. If the female figure drives the plot forward because of her sexual vulnerability and because of her resonance within the hugely popular genre of women's fiction, she also introduces elements and themes of nationalism insofar as she produces the future generations of Americans who will have to contend with slavery's aftermath. Thus, the aim of this study is to raise questions of nationalism within a debate that has focused on gender as womanhood.

Of course, the vexations of the term *mulatto* derive not just from gender considerations but from racial classifications as well. Widely believed to be derived from "mule," Werner Sollors has noted that it may also come from the Arabic word *muwallad*, meaning "mestizo" or "mixed." Though it usually designates the offspring of a black parent and a white parent, it is just as common in "tragic mulatto" narratives for the "fraction of black blood" to be more removed, thus invoking such terms as *quadroon* or *octoroon*.[14] In her comparative study of coercive interracialism in Victorian culture, Jennifer DeVere Brody remarks on the suspect and ambiguous nature of these expressions, which she concludes "tell us little or nothing about the so-called woman of color's status as slave or free, nor do the labels easily correspond with 'colors,' which are figurative, subjective, imprecise, and culturally constructed." Brody coins the neologism "mulattaroon" as a means of calling attention to such linguistic failings and underscoring their function "as a figment of the concept of pigment."[15] While I am in absolute agreement with Brody's political objectives in adopting the designation, my concern is not with the mimetic realism or meaningfulness of this nineteenth-century idiom in the social realm so much as it is with its signifying power as a literary trope, a recurrent device that places a more or less coherent body of literature into an ongoing dialogic relation. *The "Tragic Mulatta" Revisited* concerns itself with the ways in which abolitionist writers have variously deployed the term and the character to scrutinize the coextensive categories of race and nation. While my interest is the mulatta narrative, I will alternate, when appropriate, between the masculine and feminine forms of the noun throughout this study, in part to acknowledge the long and controversial history of the universalized masculine phrase "tragic mulatto." I will typically employ the masculine form when alluding to the literary tradition and the feminine form when discussing a particular instance of the trope. At the same time, I will designate with the use of scare quotes the term's status as a politically contested textual contrivance.

For all its problematic formal and narrative significations, the motif of the mixed-race female slave constitutes a central and indispensable element of antislavery reform literature. An examination into how the figure functions in the context of these identifications reveals moments in which the light-skinned character exhibits a liberatory potential in addition to reflecting the prevailing social order. Through both narrative strategy and characterization, writers in the tradition employ the device as an agent of social change as much as an emblem of victimization. For all their positional differences, they share a political sensibility and a literary vision that are forward looking—even utopian, for some—in their emphasis on contemplating the viability of an interracial republic.

Regardless of the racial ancestry of the author, the typical plot summary of such writings involves the story of an educated light-skinned heroine whose white benefactor and paramour (sometimes also the young woman's father) dies, leaving her to the auction block and/or the sexual designs of a malevolent creditor. The protagonist, sheltered from the outside world, is driven to desperation by her predicament and perhaps to an early death.[16] While this sketch describes the plot's basic outlines, writers incorporate important—though less conspicuous—interventions and complications into this schematic. At the same time as "tragic mulatto" narratives lend themselves to imaginative representations of the nation's future racial composition, the figure itself is conventionally motherless. Since mulatta narratives are generally regarded as belonging to the larger literary genre of nineteenth-century sentimental or "women's" fiction, it is predictable that they would follow many of the plot devices set out by Nina Baym in *Woman's Fiction: A Guide to Novels by and about Women in America, 1820–1870*. One characteristic of the "overplot" of such works is that the heroine is somehow abandoned. Either she is an orphan outright or she "only thinks herself to be one, or has by necessity been separated from her parents for an indefinite time."[17] To the standard plot design of women's fiction is thus added the overlay of slavery, miscegenation, and the prevailing crisis over national identity, making the figure the perfect emblem for exploring racial hybridity amid a newly "motherless" and embattled body politic.

In *Neither White Nor Black Yet Both*, Werner Sollors notes that early examples of miscegenation fiction featured "biracial founding couples" in a colonial setting. Over time, he writes, "the rise of the figures that have become known collectively as the 'Tragic Mulatto'" was accompanied by a shift in the characterization and plot of such works to a multigenerational focus and a progression "to biracial descendants, from parents to their children, and from slavery to race."[18] Put differently, the growth of the Republic and the concomitant crises surrounding racial and national formations at midcentury coincided with a coalescing of the "tragic mulatto" genre around an emblem that could encompass this constellation of concerns. Indeed, only the sexual vulnerability of a mixed-race female subject and the reproductive potential she represents and enacts within the plot allow her literally to personify the anxieties and fantasies about the ascendant nation's interracial future. If, as Malcolmson asserts, the mulatta is uniquely situated to be "the figure in whom racial sameness and difference concentrated," then she, more than her light-skinned male counterpart, can best act as a conduit for imaginative representations that reveal the multigenerational implications and contradictions for an increasingly multiracial America founded on ideals of individual liberty.[19]

To be sure, the disparate racial positionings of such foundational writers as Lydia Maria Child, William Wells Brown, Harriet Beecher Stowe, and Harriet Wilson are fundamental to their distinctive imaginative visions about how to respond to prevailing cultural tensions. Yet American literary history has ironically enacted its own form of segregation in its failure to explore the deeply imbricated nature of these writers' works across racial lines. Boundaries have been erected whereby texts authored by white abolitionist writers are almost always looked at through the prism of sentimental fiction, while black writers who employ the mulatta trope are seen almost exclusively in relation to their position in the canon of African American literature. While I recognize the racialized nature of writers' subject positions, we cannot effectively understand the tradition of miscegenation fiction by reinforcing an interpretive system that perpetuates artificial textual barriers. Rather, such authors must be properly examined in dynamic relation to one another and as hallmarks of an enduring legacy.

The contours of that legacy were largely mapped out by the generation of feminist literary critics who devoted themselves in the 1980s to recuperating the works of abolitionist writers even as they pointed to their complicity in perpetuating racial and sexual stereotypes over credible representations of lived experience. As Ann duCille has observed, African Americanist critics, in the case of William Wells Brown's *Clotel; or, The President's Daughter*, have taken the trope and its author to task for failing to walk "the party line of the black experience." That is, they disparage the convention for its divergence from "authentic" representations of black identity.[20] Other leading critics of sentimental fiction have emphasized the degree to which portrayals of the mulatta reinforce prevailing patriarchal norms. Illustratively, Jean Fagan Yellin has charged that the figure "appears to endorse the patriarchal ideology of true womanhood in relation to women of color."[21] In a similar vein, Carolyn L. Karcher has denounced the device for perpetuating "an ideology relegating people of color and white women to subordinate status."[22] The "tragic mulatta" is thus attacked for ascribing to black women the same lack of agency endured by white women under the ideological yoke of "true womanhood."

While a necessary and illuminating corrective at the time, duCille and others have since begun to move beyond such evaluative political judgments to study the multifarious cultural work the emblem performed. We can thus grant the power inherent in hegemonic regimes of antebellum racism and patriarchy and still contend that if the trope "perpetuates" such ideologies on one level, it can also be said to expose them on another. That is, we can at once acknowledge the limitations of the tradition without minimizing its success at depicting the brutal sexual subjugation of the defenseless slave/daughter by the slave-holding master/father. We can investigate not just those limitations but also the potentialities the figure evokes surrounding the contested ideological terrain of interraciality and nationhood in the decades just preceding and immediately following the Civil War.[23] Scrutinizing the works of black and white writers together can illuminate the wide variation in representational perspectives available within the same emblem.

The avowed aspiration of antislavery writers of both races was to compel their readers to imagine their own bodies as well as the body politic as ineluctably interracial. For them, light-skinned characters operated as a "rhetorical device and a political strategy" deployed, as duCille argues, to "insinuate into the consciousness of white readers the humanity of a people they otherwise constructed as subhuman—beyond the pale of white comprehension."[24] Responding to critics who label William Wells Brown's fiction assimilationist, duCille advocates reading his work with greater generosity: "What these quick condemnations too often represent, in my view, is a dangerous kind of prescriptive, anachronistic criticism that insists on reading texts not in terms of the particular social conditions, crises, and imperatives of their own historical moments but through the enlightened political sensibilities of our own. So treated, how could they not be found wanting?"[25]

Following duCille, I contend that too often such early works in the tradition of miscegenation fiction have been the victim of a similar critical misstep, which has worked to discourage inquiries into the tradition's multivalent cultural operations. Rather than realizing the full hermeneutic potential of this early figure of American racial hybridity, critics have enacted a historical displacement in which anxieties about appropriating the voice of the racialized "other" are projected backward temporally, in the process doing a disservice to the actual subjects of study. In addition, too often the new historicist trend of seeing texts as always already co-opted takes political precedence over an approach that allows for a more layered, multivalent notion of representational possibilities. Responding to this tendency, Wai-Chee Dimock has counseled against readings that, through "an act of historical repression," try to "lock the text into a single posture . . . of either opposition or containment."[26] Some criticism of the "tragic mulatto" has likewise directed an overdetermined, programmatic gaze onto a body of literature that deserves a less presentist, more expansive consideration. In the process, the tradition is denied the very complexity with which feminist critics regard the broader genre of sentimental literature.

Hazel Carby remains one of the few commentators to probe the cultural intricacies associated with the disputed figure. Writing about late-nineteenth-century works, she observed in

1987 that "the dominance of the mulatto figure in Afro-American fiction during this period has too often been dismissed as politically unacceptable without a detailed analysis of its historical and narrative function." Viewing the trope as a "narrative device of mediation," she proceeded to call for reconsiderations that would examine "what the mulatto *enabled* black authors to represent."[27] This study takes up Carby's challenge to view the motif as a narrative lens through which to explore antislavery writers' contested versions of race and nation at one of the most critical turning points in the drama of American self-definition. As Etienne Balibar avers, "[P]eoplehood is not merely a construct but one which, in each particular instance, has constantly changing boundaries." A liminal figure like the mulatta, therefore, is well situated to reveal writers'—and therefore the culture's—conflicted visions of national and racial exclusion and belonging.[28] In this way, the figure operates in various and sometimes antithetical ways to signify the depth of the social and political disruptions antebellum America was facing in the coextensive arenas of racial formation and national expansion.

Put differently, the trope enables writers of both races to capture and condense their complicated and internally contending responses to a range of intersecting crises of subjectivity at midcentury. This confluence of effects is particularly conspicuous in the case of Brown's *Clotel*, published in London in 1853. The novel, which furthered the belief that Jefferson fathered slave children, features one of the more recognizable "tragic mulattoes" in the title character of Clotel.[29] Her dramatic decision to end her life rather than return to servitude implicates one of the "Founding Fathers" in a shocking scene of self-destruction and suggests that American identity is both interracial and tragic from its earliest beginnings. Clotel, the "tragic mulatta," both embodies that inescapable fact of American history and, significantly, anticipates and prefigures a series of unmistakably rebellious events. The novel's conclusion depicts the reunion of

Clotel's daughter and her mixed-race beloved not in the North—as is the case in much antislavery fiction—but in Dunkirk, France. The couple resume their lives on the Continent, representing Brown's deliberate repudiation of his homeland and the construction of an interracial nation elsewhere. Here, then, blackness and interraciality are seen as antithetical to U.S. national allegiance, even—or perhaps especially—for descendants of a Founding Father. The author confirms his sense of national alienation in a direct address at the end of the novel, calling on his newfound compatriots to "let the voice of the whole British nation be heard across the Atlantic . . . to proclaim the Year of Jubilee."[30] Recall here that Brown himself was a fugitive who won manumission through the efforts of his British allies and returned home to the United States only reluctantly after a European speaking tour in 1854.

Harriet Wilson's *Our Nig* (1859) also draws from the "tragic mulatto" tradition to dramatize the theme of miscegenation as it bisects issues of national division and dispossession. This is evident in the title alone, which invokes the Lincolnesque image of a "house divided" in its subtitle, *Sketches from the Life of a Free Black, in a Two-Story White House, North, Showing That Slavery's Shadows Fall Even There.*[31] Wilson's is the first antislavery novel explicitly to thematize the depredations associated with the Northern wage-labor system and its interpenetration with questions of racial stratification and national allegiance. *Our Nig*, the earliest known novel published by a woman of color in the United States, both extends and supplements the slave narrative and sentimental conventions from which it emerges, in part by gesturing toward a countermodel of interracial inclusion and national belonging exemplified in the portrait of Miss Marsh, the public school teacher who appears briefly, but importantly, at the center of the work. The civic values she espouses have their origins in the sweeping nationalist ideology that marks the common school reform movement of the period, though her vision implicitly critiques the Protestant conformity of that program by embracing race and class difference.[32] The nationalism of Lydia Maria Child and Harriet Beecher Stowe is more absolute to the extent that in their fiction, the preservation of the Union is finally of paramount concern. Still, for Child, such preservation is explicitly linked to racial intermixture, whereas Stowe famously resorts to a colonizationist resolution to the dilemma of Southern slavery and racial discord.[33] Nonetheless, even here, through the deployment of narrative strategies involving the mulatta character, these authors succeed—if only provisionally—in giving voice to a decidedly radical sensibility with which the reader is invited to identify.

Although they were widely read, abolitionist writings that dared to depict interracial sex were regarded as scandalous or militant—or both. After white reformer Richard Hildreth issued *The Slave; or, Memoirs of Archy Moore* (1836), for example, the *Boston Daily Atlas*, the author's former employer, fumed: "We cannot too much deprecate the publication of such works. We are aware of no purpose which they can answer, save that of sustaining and impelling a dangerous experiment."[34] Despite the explicit intent of such works to generate popular revulsion toward the sexual servitude intrinsic to the slave system, readers commonly viewed the genre as promoting miscegenation to the extent that its mixed-race exemplars are portrayed sympathetically. Child, aware that the theme of interracial sexuality in "Slavery's Pleasant Homes" would offend a segment of her genteel readership, chose to publish the story only in an annual antislavery giftbook (the *Liberty Bell* in 1843), rather than even attempt to include it in her 1846 commercial collection, *Fact and Fiction*.[35] Karcher has underscored the politically incendiary nature of this "masterpiece" of antislavery fiction, praising its "penetrating insights into the interlocking systems of racial and sexual oppression." On the other hand, she and other twentieth-century commentators have argued that, in the words of Karen

Sánchez-Eppler, "[t]he difficulty of preventing moments of identification from becoming acts of appropriation constitutes the essential dilemma of feminist-abolitionist rhetoric."[36] In other words, the sympathy generated on the basis of gender between white female reader and black female character is overshadowed by the degree to which the mulatta figure is placed in the service of the codes of behavior of "true womanhood." In this view, the price of cross-gender identification is black subjugation and assimilation to norms of white domesticity.[37] This line of critique dates back to 1937, when Sterling Brown charged that the convention represented a "dangerous concession" to "race snobbishness" among abolitionists. He noted that audiences would be more inclined to identify with protagonists who looked like them and argued that "the superiority wished upon the octoroons was easily attributed to the white blood coursing in their veins, and the white audience was thereby flattered."[38] Brown's position was solidly grounded in the racial "uplift" ethos of his historical moment.

In our own day, one of the reasons for critics' reluctance to reevaluate the role of the "tragic mulatto" is its inextricable connection with domestic fiction, which has been under renewed attack of late since its brief recuperation by Jane Tompkins and other feminist critics in the mid-1980s.[39] Most influentially, Lauren Berlant has revived the long-standing charge that the very individualized and personal nature of sentimental narrative renders it incapable of addressing structural reform in the political realm: "Because the ideology of true feeling cannot admit the nonuniversality of pain," Berlant asserts, "its causes become all jumbled together and the ethical imperative toward social transformation is replaced by a civic-minded but passive ideal of empathy."[40] While this critique may be sound in relation to our own postmodern literary sensibility, it denies nineteenth-century sentimental fiction its essential grounding in a particularized historical and cultural milieu and in so doing deprives it of its potentially transgressive effects upon its contemporaneous readership.

In her response to critics like Berlant, who accuse turn-of-the-century "tragic mulatto" stories with inducing political docility, Susan Gilman has argued for a broader understanding of racial "melodramas" that encompass "varying imaginary resolutions to an array of social contradictions" reflecting conflicting demands of racial, sexual, and national identities. She has insisted that such resolutions "differ as dramatically, and significantly, as do the formulations of the problems facing the black race in white America."[41] Indeed, it seems puzzling to suggest that domestic fiction could be devoid of the same degree of complex and contested political valences accorded other forms of popular fiction in nineteenth-century America. It is a truism in critical theory, of course, that texts and literary traditions both reflect and shape the existing social order. At the same time, I heed Dana Nelson's caution that it is wrong to see power "as only oppressive. It can be productive and progressive—both by the intentions of those who exercise it, and unintentionally in the gaps left by its constant failure to create a total, seamless whole."[42] In the texts under discussion here, then, the mixed-race female exemplar at moments enacts a transgressive role even within the structures of power that constrain her. She functions both as an oppositional figure in her capacity to challenge existing racial boundaries and as a device that enables authors to work through their sometimes contradictory sentiments about pressing questions of national identity.

Many critics of the convention overlook the fact that such white writers as Child, Hildreth, and Stowe were themselves responding to an existing legacy of Southern plantation fiction that they were in part endeavoring to critique. Under these literary conventions, slaves were commonly represented as lazy and ignorant, and the institution of slavery was championed as a necessary and benevolent one. Even in the North prior to the

1830s, publications by colonizationists and gradualists, as well as proslavery apologists, all reinforced the protective nature of the slave system. The brutality of the institution was rarely represented, nor did there appear depictions of slaves as morally or intellectually capable of freedom. Mason Stokes views this tradition of "plantation romances" as a "shifting, complicated, yet continuous record of how white Americans lived and commodified racist ideologies" in the period. While the specter of miscegenation is certainly central to this strain of popular literature, it surfaces most often in connection with the sexual threat posed by the black male. Stokes remarks on the relative absence in these narratives of black women, whose presence would, of necessity, make unavoidable some degree of acknowledgment of white masculinist complicity in the perceived threat to white women's racial "purity."[43]

By virtue of their divergent political objectives and their shared literary tradition, Northern abolitionist writers have as their explicit subject of scrutiny—in a way absent from proslavery writings—the offspring of illicit sexual liaisons between members of the white planter class and their female slaves. The writers I address were among those most prominent in institutionalizing the sympathetic portrayal of the mixed-race heroine. They undertook to follow accepted fictional forms while challenging white supremacist representations of racial politics under slavery. As I've indicated, these writers were heavily influenced by one another across racial boundaries. In fact, as we shall discover, in *Clotel*, Brown went so far as to reproduce whole sections of Child's early stories. Even Stowe's masterwork bears clear signs of having been inspired by both Child and Hildreth and, of course, a host of slave narratives. In some ways, therefore, the "tragic mulatto" tradition can be seen as a highly cohesive and mutually constitutive one. On less explicit levels, however, writers in this genre struggled in diverse ways with the overlapping issues of national and racial identity that were consuming the Republic. Each of them offers varied and often internally conflicted responses to this challenge to American self-definition, and for each the "tragic mulatto" embodies the central medium for their exploration.

Each chapter of *The "Tragic Mulatto" Revisited* juxtaposes contemporaneous historical and political events with a discussion of a writer's rendering of the mulatta exemplar to suggest the degree to which these representations were shaped by such events, no matter how indirectly. Prior studies of the figure tend to stay within the literary historical realm of sentimental fiction in their discussions. Widening the contextual frame in this study emphasizes what Sarah Chinn describes as "concurrent but contingent cultural phenomena, spoken into being together by culture."[44] In the process, it demonstrates the wide-ranging explorations of nationalism and interraciality carried out within and through the "tragic mulatto" device. Thus, the first chapter discusses the works of perhaps the most widely known popularizer of the genre, Lydia Maria Child, within the broad cultural context of scientific and romantic racialism, as well as the ascendant rhetoric of nationalism and manifest destiny. Child's various depictions of interraciality, involving both Native Americans and "tragic quadroons," constitute her conflicted response to these discursive regimes.

In her earliest novel, *Hobomok, A Tale of Early Times* (1824), Child first turns to the trope of miscegenation as a rhetorical device to prompt her readers to consider an alternative social order. *Hobomok* offers the beginnings of a developing critique of racism that nonetheless falters to the degree that it endorses an expansionist notion of American national and cultural supremacy. This complex narrative trajectory, interrogating, as it does, ideologies of white supremacy and manifest destiny, appears for the first time in *Hobomok* and recurs consistently in Child's later abolitionist work as well. In her antislavery stories of the 1840s, Child's narrative strategy challenged readers to redefine prevailing notions of both private and national "family" to embrace their interracial members. In Child's 1843 story "Slavery's Pleasant Homes," for example, Rosa, the light-skinned slave who is also the half-sister of her mistress, is driven to sexual servitude and an early death after giving birth to her master/father's child. Rosa's death is then avenged by her lover and fellow slave, George, who murders his master—who is also his half-brother. The plot is resolutely tangled and melodramatic not only to expose the victimization and descent into violence the slave system encourages in both white and black families but also to compel readers to question prevailing assumptions about the racial configuration of the antebellum slave-holding family itself. The story's ironic title gestures not only to the violence inherent to the institution but also to the interracial domestic space. Finally, Child sees the miscegenated Southern family not as alien to but as implicated in the larger American family, in-eluctably interconnected and mutually constitutive. At the same time, the efficacy of the reformer's progressive interventions are weighed against her impulse to embrace hegemonic ideologies of U.S. national ascendancy. In this regard, I examine Child's little-known work "Willie Wharton," an 1863 narrative about Anglo–American Indian interracial marriage and assimilation, as well as *A Romance of the Republic*, Child's postbellum novel. Here, Child draws on the "tragic mulatto" again to portray a so-cial order that is both multiracial and egalitarian. It is undoubt-edly her most utopian and most ambitious literary undertaking, though it also betrays her anxiety about the ability of the newly reconstructed Union to preserve its nationalist project.[45]

Whereas Child often uses the mixed-race heroine to posit a world of racial diversity in which the interracial family stands in for the interracial nation, William Wells Brown employs the de-vice to disturb the very categories at work in the construction of U.S. ideologies of national origin and identity. In chapter 2, I show how he simultaneously appropriates Child's antislavery stories and diverges distinctively from them to comment upon contemporary ideas at the intersection of miscegenation and nationalism. The premise that Clotel's paternity stretches back to the nation's founding constitutes on ongoing rebuke to the ideals of the Revolution and suggests that Americanness is coextensive with interraciality from the Republic's earliest origins. Throughout his novel, Brown deploys a complex overlay of historical material—documentary and imaginative—that interrupts and frustrates the linear "tragic mulatto" narrative in a pastiche of literary styles. For example, he paraphrases from a purported newspaper account describing Senator Daniel Webster being mistaken for a black man in a railway car. Elsewhere, he recounts the case of a German immigrant girl taken into slavery and cites a supposed journalistic report of a court proceeding in which the judge rules that judicial "smelling powers" shall determine race.[46] In such narrative interludes as these, Brown satirizes emerging "scientific" methods—including the 1850 census—to delineate and circumscribe racial categories. The fact that several of these episodes evoke cherished democratic institutions—the courtroom, the Senate—further underscores the hypocrisy at the root of the nation's founding principles. By thus manipulating political discourse, as well as those of sentimentalist and reform rhetoric, Brown challenges readers' conceptions of both American nationalism and the "naturalness" of racial identity. In the imaginary resolution of the novel, which portrays the next generation of Jefferson's progeny renouncing their homeland, national affiliation becomes as porous a category as race.

Like Brown's *Clotel*, the white reformer Richard Hildreth's novel *The Slave; or, Memoirs of Archy Moore* (1836) was one of many sources of influence for Stowe's *Uncle Tom's Cabin*, along with slave narratives and Theodore Weld's 1839 collection of slaveholder accounts, *American Slavery As It Is*.[47] The third chapter contends that Hildreth's novel can be thought of as a precursor to Stowe's masterwork that participated in what Robert B. Stepto has termed an ongoing "antislavery textual conversation" with the later novel.[48] Hildreth's contribution to this narrative dialogue was unprecedented in its presentation of mixed-race characters who could successfully mediate between militancy and gentility while still enjoying the sympathy of readers. Indeed, the two works have often been compared to one another both for their artistry and their "inflammatory effects" on public opinion.[49] In what would soon become a familiar theme of interracial sexual coercion, the title character and his wife, Cassy, are both the offspring of Colonel Moore, the patriarch of a Virginia plantation. When the colonel is thwarted in his attempt to subdue Cassy sexually only by the unexpected return of his legitimate white family, Cassy exclaims to her husband, "Oh Archy—and he my father!"[50]

Here, writing sixteen years before Stowe, Hildreth tackles not only the subject of the sexual exploitation inherent under slavery but the complex and interpenetrated issues of miscegenation and incest in a plantation context. He dramatizes the paradox in which proportions of "blood" are metaphorized and quantified as race, only to be used to deny relations of kinship. More broadly, such scenes challenge readers to question who is to be included and excluded as citizens in the national body politic. Hildreth's Cassy qualifies as an early representative of the "tragic mulatto" tradition given her parentage and the sexual subjugation with which she is threatened, though she never occupies the centerpiece of the plot in the same way as later manifestations of the character. Thus, *The Slave* was both one of the first antislavery novels to deploy a mixed-race heroine and the first whose narrative championed violent overthrow rather than meek submission to tyranny.

Following this discussion of the figure of the mulatta in one of Stowe's most important textual influences, I turn to an examination of its conflicted role in *Uncle Tom's Cabin* (1852). In

addition to Hildreth's influence, Lydia Maria Child's importance
to the genre manifests itself in an early chapter of Stowe's masterwork titled "The Quadroon's Story." Echoing Child's 1843
tale "The Quadroons," the chapter recounts Cassy's ill-fated life
before she finds herself the slave and sexual concubine of the
baleful slaveholder Simon Legree. While this autobiographical
sketch of Cassy's life accords with the conventional narrative
trajectory of the doomed mulatta heroine, the way in which her
character functions within the plot of the novel is much more
complex and polysemous.[51] This underexamined figure is the
mastermind behind the elaborately staged "haunting" of Legree,
during which she engineers her own escape as well as that of
her fellow slave Emmeline, before her conversion to Christian
piety. Only then is Cassy suddenly transformed into a voiceless,
passive vessel of Protestant devotion in a move that suggests
more is at work than just the conventional Christian conversion
narrative that accompanies Tom's death. Despite critics' charge
of the "tragic mulatto's" passivity, Stowe invests Cassy with a dynamic sense of agency, at least as she is first presented to us. In
that both novels feature mulattas of the same name, a radical
sensibility can be traced from Hildreth's earlier text to its manifestation in Stowe's most insurrectionary character.

If only provisionally, therefore, Cassy operates as both the
most threatening exemplar in *Uncle Tom's Cabin* of the fact of
miscegenation and, because of her gendered history, the most
militant vehicle for its continued reproduction. Of course, the
mixed-race status of the entire family is elided and its national
identity transmuted in George Harris's final identification with
"the oppressed, enslaved African race."[52] Here, Stowe's containment of the mulatto figure's radical potential both reflects and
invokes a growing national anxiety about the sociopolitical effects of increasing racial intermixture. The disequilibrium in
Cassy's figuration thus functions to expose a larger tension regarding the degree to which the Republic was willing to ac-

knowledge its changing body politic, its newly recognized racial hybridity. Thus, rather than condemn it as a formulaic, politically retrograde literary device, I show that for such influential abolitionist writers as Stowe, the "tragic mulatto" operates on various contending levels in response to the profound redefinitions of race and nation that were occurring at the moment of its greatest public appeal.

In chapter 4, I synthesize my interpretive concerns by positing Harriet Wilson's *Our Nig* as both an extension of and a counterpoint to the texts previously considered, especially with regard to its representation of the "tragic mulatto." More than in any other work, Wilson's mixed-race heroine directly challenges stock notions of the figure to comment on issues of interraciality and nationalism in the antebellum North. The first antislavery novel authored by an African American woman writer is also the first to incorporate a self-conscious and unrelenting critique of class inequities in the "Two-Story White House, North"—that phrase in the novel's subtitle that subtly alludes to differences of class, region, and national identity at once. The chapter begins with an analysis of the system of poor relief Wilson endured and moves to a discussion of Frado's mother's biracial marriage to argue that Wilson's novel is among the first works of reform literature to offer an integrated understanding of the operations of race and class prejudice at midcentury. Wilson both relies on and manipulates the "tragic mulatto" tradition in her representation of Frado's powerful subjectivity alongside her domestic subjugation. Fostered by the character of the broad-minded public school teacher, Miss Marsh, Frado's growing sense of self inscribes in the narrative a profoundly transformative role for the larger public sphere. Finally, I introduce an allegorical component of the text and the title to suggest that in prevailing upon her readers to accept the mulatto foundling into the "national home," Wilson is exhorting them to reconceive that home by recognizing and acknowledging the fact of interraciality. In this way, *Our Nig* represents the extent to which political and rhetorical battles over U.S. nationalism and miscegenation are construed as not only coextensive but conjoined.

The *"Tragic Mulatta" Revisited* concludes by turning to present-day reincarnations of the device to suggest some continuities amid radical revisions in America's cultural imaginings of its racial past. Here, I examine the contemporary fascination with the Sally Hemings story as exemplified by the film *Jefferson in Paris* and the CBS television miniseries *Sally Hemings: An American Scandal.*[53] As William Wells Brown first demonstrated in 1853, the story of Jefferson's long-standing liaison with his slave—and the popular furor that association fomented—constitutes the ingredients for the archetypal "tragic mulatto" tale in its interpenetrating concerns over racial and national identity. Unlike Brown's version, however, the focus in the present-day renderings is the presumed love story between the Southern planter/statesman and his bondwoman. This determined representation of a romance between "forbidden lovers" betrays an enduring American anxiety about the extent to which the nation was founded not on the lofty ideals of "life, liberty, and the pursuit of happiness" but on a history of racial and sexual brutality and subjugation. Such anxiety—and its parallel fantasy of white redemption through interracial mutual love—is enacted over the body of the updated "tragic mulatto."

By contrast, some popular novels, including the controversial parody *The Wind Done Gone*, set out self-consciously to undermine and supercede the "tragic mulatto" tradition. In Alice Randall's recent best seller, Cynara, Mammy's mixed-race daughter, becomes the controlling figure of the narrative. As she gains her voice and her agency, it is Cynara who eventually abandons the aging Rhett Butler analogue for a dashing Reconstruction-era congressman. More than that, the aim of *The Wind Done Gone* is to expose the depths of interracial intimacy under plantation slavery that are masked by the romantic fantasy of Southern domestic chivalry. Every major female character in the parody turns out to have black ancestry, revealing the invented and ideological nature of biological racial distinctions. In Randall's maternalist re-creation, the story of American race history becomes the story of cross-racial mother love. The ubiquitous mixed-race woman is therefore evidence *of* and vehicle *for* the reproduction of racial indeterminacy. Finally, Randall suggests, the mulatta stands as a figure for the quintessential American in her gendered racial hybridity.

The mulatta trope fell victim in the 1980s to a strain of feminist literary criticism that demanded of nineteenth-century women's fiction a more or less univocal stance of resistance to hegemonic ideologies. Since then, such commentators as Rita Felski have recognized that "popular fiction can more usefully be read as comprising a variety of ideological strands that cohere to or contradict each other in diverse ways."[54] *The "Tragic Mulatta" Revisited* is meant to surmount literary critics' repudiation of the figure by demonstrating that it encompasses just such ideological complexities and that those complexities can help us reconfigure the workings of race and nation in antebellum literature and culture. While Ann Cvetkovich is astute in her observation that an intervention within literary or cultural studies "is not always a synecdoche for other forms of resistance," it is also true that a project that reconceives a contested figure in American literary history can be useful—in a heuristic, if not a political sense—at a time when the United States is becoming increasingly multiracial even as it faces intensifying antagonism toward its own changing character.[55]

CHAPTER 1

Of Romances and Republics in Lydia Maria Child's Miscegenation Fiction

IN RECENT YEARS, feminist criticism has restored Lydia Maria Child to her rightful place next to Harriet Beecher Stowe as perhaps the second-most widely read and influential writer and reformer of the mid-nineteenth century. She has been heralded with virtually inventing several prose genres, among them American children's literature, the journalistic sketch, and the domestic advice book.[1] However, along with Stowe, the antislavery activist and writer has been assailed for succumbing to romantic racialism in her representations of black characters. While she did not invent the tradition that has relied upon the "tragic mulatto," no nineteenth-century writer was more instrumental in the trope's proliferation and circulation.[2] Whether in short stories for abolitionist giftbooks and literary magazines of the day or in such novels as *A Romance of the Republic*, Child was famous for making use of the refined, mixed-race slave to garner support first for emancipation and then for civil and social acceptance. In critical assessments today, Child is seen as a prime example of writers who, in Jean Fagan Yellin's words, allowed "white readers to identify with the victim by gender while distancing themselves by race and thus to avoid confronting a racial ideology that denies the full humanity of nonwhite women."[3] That is, the mulatta narrative encouraged identification along the axis of gender at the same time as it ultimately disavowed cross-racial allegiances.

While acknowledging the problematic workings of female characterization of any type in sentimental fiction, I want to question the orthodox denunciation of a genre that performs such multifarious ideological operations. If it is true, as we have come to understand from so many contemporary theorists, that such identity categories as race and gender cannot be isolated but instead express themselves through and in the terms of one another, then how is it possible for readers not to see themselves mirrored in racial as well as gendered terms in these narratives? For the tales to have accomplished their rhetorical aims, how could they not have called on their audience to identify with their heroines in *all* aspects of their subjectivities? Indeed, how better could an antislavery writer reach her or his audience than through a figure that, according to the prevailing racial logic of the day, embodied the one-drop rule? This chapter seeks to widen the angle of vision regarding the cultural and racial function of the mulatta in Child's literary productions, especially as these intersect with questions of national identity. First, however, to understand more fully the symbolic and rhetorical import of the recurring device, it is necessary to explore some of the social and historical preconditions for its existence.

In her work on antebellum "projects of resistance," Maggie Sale discusses the need to "rematerialize the context in which [the writer's sentimental] strategies were originally produced and articulated."[4] Contemporary criticism of the "tragic mulatta" tends to project backward a transhistorical and fixed sense of U.S. ideologies of racial difference. In fact, the tradition employing the mulatta character came into being at the very time enduring notions of race were crystallizing in the new republic. It is instructive to recall, for example, that until early in the nineteenth century, the prevailing American intellectual view, inherited from the European Enlightenment, was not only that

all humans descended from one species but that racial difference
was attributable to environmental causes.[5] Throughout the revolutionary era, the fact of black enslavement was an embarrass-
ment to the principle of "natural rights," a contradiction that
helped abolish the international slave trade in 1807. However,
the need quickly surfaced for an ideology that would place the
responsibility for the abject condition of blacks on their own
innate deficiencies. The emergence of scientific racialism at
midcentury—in tandem with such concepts as phrenology, polygenesis, and Anglo-Saxonism—arose concurrently with America's increasing dependence on slave labor and its simultaneous
westward expansion. The ranking of races from superior to inferior that preoccupied a generation of antebellum scientists provided a perfect rationale not only for black enslavement but also
for the concomitant activities of wholesale American Indian removal and extermination to facilitate the settlement of western
territories.

This growing confidence in white racial superiority
blended with a parallel sense of providentially sanctioned nationalist destiny. During this period, the United States acquired
vast territories from Mexico and accomplished the displacement
of Native Americans across the central Plains states at the same
time as the Southern slave population was exploding. But the
ascendant republic's ambitions were internationalist as well. In
the early 1850s, the "Young Americans," an extremist but ideo-
logically influential wing of the Democratic Party, used the
rhetoric of republicanism and universal freedom to advocate expansion westward into Asia, southward to the Caribbean, and
northward to Canada. They envisioned nothing less than an
"Anglo-Saxon United States of the World."[6] Even those who
were less messianic about America's mission for world dominion
believed in the commercial promise of expansionism.

At the same time, such imperialist enthusiasm was tempered
by fears of widespread amalgamation and "racial mongreliza-

tion" with nonwhite natives. Racial theorists responded to these fears by arguing that, over time, the superior "Anglo-American race" would supplant and displace "inferior" colonized peoples. The rhetoric surrounding these conquests reveals just how embedded the new scientific racialism became in the project of nation building. The war with Mexico was justified on the grounds that "the degraded Mexican-Spanish" were morally incapable of receiving the "virtues of the Anglo-Saxon race." California was annexed thanks to the "irresistible army of Anglo-Saxon emigration."[7] Josiah C. Nott, a prominent racial theorist, was particularly preoccupied with the deleterious effects of intermixture across racial lines. An illustrious Southern surgeon who gained an international reputation for his writings defending innate black inferiority, Nott was one of the earliest, and perhaps the most important, proponents of the notion that "interbreeding" led to infertile offspring and the deterioration of the genetic stock of both parent races. The idea that mulattoes were less fertile than their progenitors lent credence to the theory of separate species and fostered the fear of the adulteration of "pure" Anglo-Saxon blood. Nott wrote that "wherever in the history of the world the inferior races have been conquered and mixed in with the Caucasian, the latter have sunk into barbarism."[8] In this way, myths about the inability of mulattoes to procreate beyond a few generations flourished alongside anxieties about the pervading contamination of whites by black "blood."

Propelled by these theories, the one-drop rule, which denied the very existence of the mixed-race subject, was rapidly embraced. Scott L. Malcolmson argues that in the nineteenth century, "[t]he Negro in his appearance marked the indelibility of American history, white and black. The Negro, then, had somehow to leave, or at a minimum to be safely contained."[9] Legislatures and courts throughout the South acted quickly to make sure that the fact of such "indelibility" was indeed

"contained." Whereas the lower South had resisted legal definitions of blackness for generations, the eruption of antimiscegenation rhetoric fueled the passage of scores of state laws
outlawing the practice. A full thirty-eight states banned interracial relationships by midcentury; some, like Louisiana, mounted
efforts to expel free people of color, most of whom were of
mixed racial heritage. Vigilante groups formed to drive free
blacks out and to police interracial liaisons of all kinds. One jury
determined that "we should have but two classes, the Master and
the Slave, and no intermediate class can be other than im-
mensely mischievous to our peculiar institution."[10] At the same
time as the ideology of racial separation was intensifying, however, the evidence of accelerating racial intermixture became increasingly inescapable. As Joel Williamson points out, "It was
everywhere evident that slavery was getting whiter and whiter,
and that planter men bore a significant part of the responsibility
for that trend"—no matter how incongruous it was with prevailing public opinion. After all, a growing slave population was
necessary in the 1840s and 1850s for the institution's westward
expansion. According to Williamson: "The fact that slavery was
getting whiter, that in reality many slaves were more white than
black, was a fact with which the proslavery argument could not
cope. Either it could ignore the problem, which it did explicitly,
or it could brusquely dismiss it by applying the one-drop rule to
persons in slavery, which it did implicitly."[11]

Not coincidentally, then, the "tragic mulatto" figure appears
in fiction just at this moment of acute disjuncture between the
avowed ideology of the one-drop rule and the inescapably interracial nature of antebellum Southern life. Here it is useful to recall Hazel Carby's delineation of the mulatta emblem's narrative
purpose: "[H]istorically the mulatto, as narrative figure, has two
primary functions: as a vehicle for an exploration of the relationship between the races and, at the same time, an expression
of the relationship between the races."[12] More than a simple

mirror of some "objective" state of affairs in the social sphere, the literary mulatta operates on another level as a medium through which Child and other antislavery writers could investigate the implications of their contradictory cultural surroundings. Indeed, the device can be seen as the most logical literary response available with which to interrogate the inextricable discourses of racial and national incorporation.

HOBOMOK AND THE "YENGEES"

Child's sustained interest in the mulatta flows naturally from her earliest writings, which are self-consciously alive to the synchronous issues of miscegenation and nationalism. Because her first novel anticipates the concerns so central to her antislavery work, a discussion of its key elements is useful here, despite its setting in Puritan New England instead of the antebellum South. Carolyn L. Karcher has charted the young writer's dependence upon and departure from an emerging tradition of American literary nationalism that included James Fenimore Cooper, along with less canonical authors. In 1824, when Child undertook to write *Hobomok, A Tale of Early Times*, she was responding to Cooper's insistent denial of interracial sex in his imaginative vision. As well, she was answering a call from critics "to explore the matchless resources that America's panoramic landscapes, heroic Puritan settlers, and exotic Indian folklore afforded the romancer."[13] While *Hobomok* shares the theme of interracial romance with its predecessors, Karcher points out that it differs importantly in its critique of white supremacy. It constitutes the first of scores of fictional interventions designed not only to entertain but also to proffer a reconstructed social order capacious enough to welcome mixed-race unions. The novel marks the first time Child will turn to the motif of miscegenation as a vehicle for working through conflicting racial and national imperatives. It offers a developing critique of racist ideological structures that nonetheless falters to the degree that it endorses a hegemonic notion of Anglo-American national ascendancy.

Hobomok takes as its subject the life of "Naumkeak," a seventeenth-century Puritan settlement "on the eastern shore of Massachusetts."[14] Judging from much of the commentary about the work, one would assume that the theme of miscegenation dominates every page.[15] In reality, the marriage of young Mary Conant—presumed to be widowed—to the devoted Native American scout, Hobomok, does not occur until three-quarters of the way through the story. Overlooked in the scholarship is a dimension that deserves greater consideration for its centrality both to Child's politics and her art. The greatest portion of the tale is concerned with issues of spirituality and the characters' relation to orthodox Puritanism. Child's own youthful departure from the Congregationalist Church and her growing affinity for various transcendentalist ideas are developments that are intimately connected with her evolving political and literary sensibilities. The plot signals the centrality of such questions to Child in its preoccupation with religious rhetoric and doctrine.

Mary's father, Mr. Conant, is a stern Calvinist who appears to stand in for Child's own harsh father. The character whose religious views receive the greatest opportunity for expression is the village's new "nonconformist" minister, Francis Higginson. In a ceremony celebrating his arrival, Higginson delivers a sermon remarkably similar to the teachings of Emanuel Swedenborg, the eighteenth-century Swedish mystic popular among religious radicals of Child's day: "The first use I would make of the office wherewithal I am honored, is to say to you, talk little about religion, and feel much of its power. Follow the light which is given you. 'Commune with your own heart, and be still.'"[16] The unattributed quotation concluding Higginson's injunction intensifies the sense that Child, through the novel's seventeenth-century minister, is articulating sentiments that won't become fashionable until they are uttered by the transcendentalist figures of Swedenborg and Ralph Waldo Emerson. In fact, Child first learned of the teachings of Swedenborg as a youngster in Norridgewock, Maine, at the same time as she learned to appreciate the heritage of the Abenaki and Penobscot tribes.[17] She was attracted by the transcendentalist "doctrine of correspondences," which holds that everything in the natural world is the expression of a higher spirituality, and by the optimism of a faith that believed in the innate goodness of humanity and the harmony between humanity and nature. This transcendentalist formulation would later find expression in Child's stylized portraits of mulatta figures, whose depictions would be replete with metaphors from the natural world.[18]

Yet for all her devotion to the ideas of Swedenborg, Child consistently abhorred narrow sectarianism in either politics or religion, as suggested in *Hobomok* in the sympathetic presentation of Mary's suitor, Charles Brown, an Episcopal minister and lawyer.[19] Brown arrives in the settlement to win converts to the Church of England. Instead, he wins Mary's affections and the scorn of the town's elders, who accuse him of practicing the sacrament and exile him to England. Mary is soon overwhelmed with a series of losses, including the deaths of her mother and grandfather. She also learns that the East India vessel carrying her fiancé has been shipwrecked, and Charles is presumed dead. Mary, overwrought and desolate, proposes marriage to Hobomok, a Native American scout who, as a servant, had doted on her. Initially, to foreground the progression undergone by Mary, Child casts the choice in the most negative terms possible. She extends the proposal in the context of her "desolation" and "misery" after hearing the news of Charles's demise, news that "had almost hurled reason from its throne." What is worse, she concedes that resentment at her father's coldness may have prompted her to choose the course of action she does: "Her heart writhing and convulsed as it was, was gentle still; and it now craved one expression of tenderness, one expression of love. That soothing influence she sought in vain." At the outset, intermarriage between Mary and Hobomok is linked with witchcraft, insanity, and death. Indeed, Mary's father would rather have heard that his daughter had died: "'I had made up my mind to her watery grave,' said he; 'but to have her lie in the bosom of a savage, and mingle her prayers with a heathen, who knoweth not God, is hard for a father's heart to endure.'"[20]

Such sentiments hardly seem to be the work of a budding social reformer. Yet if we dissect them carefully, it becomes clear that Mr. Conant's remarks perform various functions—some of which are at odds with each other—that can be linked to aspects of Child's social thought. On the surface, these remarks would seem to confirm and endorse the reader's most racist assumptions. At the same time, for the speech to accomplish that end, the reader would have to be utterly convinced of the truth of the following contentions: first, the extreme view that Mary's death would, indeed, be more palatable than marriage to Hobomok; and second, that Hobomok is, in fact, no more than a "savage . . . heathen, who knoweth not God." Accepting these propositions requires the reader to ignore the cognitive dissonance that follows from the fact of Hobomok's evident refinement and unwavering devotion to his troubled wife: "Hobomok continued the same tender reverence he had always evinced, and he soon understood the changing expression of her countenance, till her very looks were a law."[21] Rejecting the father's contentions, on the other hand, would entail, at the least, questioning the virtues of his doctrinaire Calvinism. This, to be sure, is one of Child's aims. More broadly, such a rejection would propel the reader into the unstable position of aligning herself or himself for the moment with the point of view of the "savage."

A similar rhetorical operation is performed when, after marrying Hobomok, Mary laments that "her own nation looked upon her as lost and degraded; and what was far worse, her own heart echoed back the charge."[22] Presumably, the reader's sympathy with Mary's bereaved state of mind precludes her from characterizing the story's heroine as "degraded." However, granting that degree of identification necessarily places the reader in the odd position of being excluded, in some sense, from the collectivity defined as "her own nation." That distancing effect of the reader from received opinion is intensified with the turn in the next sentence toward Mary's internalizing such negative opinion. The phrase "far worse," then, carries a double referent: Not only does Mary's internalization of racism lead to the intensification of her pain, the reader's newfound affinity for both Mary and Hobomok increases the feeling of discomfort at witnessing the cruel effects of such internalization, which the reader may previously have been guilty of producing and perpetuating.

The foregoing anatomization of the rhetorical work of the narrative is meant to convey a sense of Child's careful approach to the project of ideological persuasion. In 1839, she would describe her rhetorical style as attacking "bigotry" with "a troop of horse shod with felt; that is, I try to *enter* the wedge of general principles, letting inferences unfold themselves very gradually."[23] Child's prose does not challenge so much as it performs an act of political seduction. For her, fiction, especially stories for children, "should be written with a view to bring the moral emotions into activity."[24] Thus, when Mary comments about Hobomok that "every day I live with that kind, noble-hearted creature, the better I love him," the reader is meant to share in Mary's feelings of respect and appreciation.

The novel ends with a restoration of the social order, but with a significant difference: the appearance of perhaps the first offspring of an interracial couple in American literature. Mary and Hobomok give birth to a son, named Charles Hobomok Conant after Mary's long-lost betrothed. However, when Charles Conant suddenly returns after being held prisoner on the African coast, Hobomok, in a gesture of sacrificial gallantry, forgoes all claims to his family and flees into the woods, making possible the climactic reunion of the estranged Anglo-American couple. The novel's conclusion recounts the educational accomplishments of the son of Mary and Hobomok, who becomes "a distinguished graduate at Cambridge" and thereafter "depart[s] to finish his studies in England." The narrator proclaims: "His [Charles Hobomok Conant's] father was seldom spoken of; and by degrees his [the son's] Indian appellation was silently omitted. But the devoted, romantic love of Hobomok was never forgotten by its object; and his faithful services to the 'Yengees' are still remembered with gratitude; though the tender slip which he protected, has since become a mighty tree, and the nations of the earth seek refuge beneath its branches."[25]

In this conclusion, it becomes apparent that Child's ability to conceive of a liberational potential for miscegenation in this early work cannot sustain itself against the powerful parallel discourse of American nationalism and expansion, in which there is little room for cultural difference. Intended to serve as a parting tribute to the "noble Indian," the passage instead enacts not only Hobomok's self-eradication but also the total assimilation and enculturation of his son. First, the son is given the Anglo name Charles even before the return of his namesake; next, his "Indian appellation" is gradually elided entirely from the family's history. In this operation of literal self-effacement, and in the final romanticized metaphor of the sapling as the budding American nation, we see a rehearsal in small of precisely the kind of subjugation and co-optation that characterized the history of U.S.–American Indian relations. Here, Hobomok is finally seen as no more than an instrument in the service of the burgeoning American empire.

As assimilationist as Child's treatment of interracial coupling in *Hobomok* seems to us, however, it was incendiary enough in its own time to provoke a hostile notice in the *North American Review*, which found the plot "unnatural" and "revolting . . . to every feeling of delicacy in man or woman."[26] Indeed, it took the intervention of an approving George Ticknor to boost sales of the novel and to secure Child's favorable reputation in Boston literary circles.[27] What makes the novel so striking historically, despite its nationalist capitulation, is its radical stance on miscegenation in comparison to other contemporaneous fiction in the same genre. Unlike Cooper's *Last of the Mohicans* and Catherine Sedgwick's *Hope Leslie*, both published shortly after Child's work, *Hobomok* features both the willing intermarriage of a white woman and an American Indian and the positive portrayal of the offspring of that union in the figure of Charles Hobomok Conant. While her contemporaries adhered to the reigning ideological injunction against violating nature by intermingling the races, Child presented interracial marriage as a potential corrective to white racial hegemony—a vision that is as problematic in our own historical moment as it was shockingly radical in pre–Civil War America. In imagining the destiny of the nation as a harmonious blend of races and cultures, Child, at age twenty-six, has prefigured the consuming focus of her later career, though she won't join the antislavery movement for several more years.[28] *Hobomok* thus sets the stage philosophically for Child's manifesto on behalf of black emancipation and social equality in *An Appeal in Favor of That Class of Americans Called Africans* (1833), a work that will continue the writer and activist's defense of intermarriage and itself make the case polemically that she will later make in the realm of literature through the device of the "tragic mulatta."

A BOLD APPEAL

While David Walker's *Appeal to the Coloured Citizens of the World* condemned slavery and colonization in 1829, Child's volume was the first printed in the United States to demand immediate emancipation and to insist on the intellectual equivalence of the races. The title of Child's treatise itself announces the author's intent to privilege the "American" identity of persons of African heritage. It also implies that the singular term "Africans," then in widespread currency, is a misnomer. Indeed, the title gestures at the tensions felt by blacks between identifications of race and "Americanness," presaging W.E.B. Du Bois's famed notion of "double consciousness." In a single stroke, then, Child reconfigures the national polity from the point of view of the minority race. On the volatile issue of "amalgamation," she writes: "In the first place, the government ought not to be invested with power to control the affections, any more than the consciences, of citizens. A man has at least as good a right to choose his wife, as he has to choose his religion. His taste may not suit his neighbors; but so long as his deportment is correct, they have no right to interfere with his concerns."[29]

This yoking of cross-racial affective freedoms with the constitutional freedoms of conscience and religion would unsettle some readers even today. More scandalous in a time when the prevailing scientific and political discourses were converging to portray blacks as genetically backward and racial mixture as dangerous to Anglo-Saxon "stock," Child proclaims miscegenation to be nothing more than a matter of social "taste." In the chapter "Colonization Society, and Anti-Slavery Society," Child rails against the colonizationists for "writing and speaking, both in public and in private," as if the "prejudice against skins darker than our own, was a fixed and unalterable law of our nature, which cannot be changed," and offers a biting critique of the one-drop rule at the same time. In a tone full of irony, she forecasts a day a hundred years in the future when "some negro Rothschild may come from Hayti, with his seventy *million* pounds, and persuade some white woman to *sacrifice* herself to him." She then poses and answers the rhetorical question: "Shall we keep this class of people in everlasting degradation, for fear one of their descendants *may* marry our great-great-great-great-grandchild? While the prejudice exists, such unions cannot take place; and when the prejudice is melted away, they will cease to be a degradation, and of course cease to be an evil."[30] Here, Child's vision turns the pervasive fear of racial comingling into a hoped-for future nation of multiracial and multiethnic harmony, an achievement she would represent in literary form in later short stories and in the 1867 novel *A Romance of the Republic*. While these works would adopt a decidedly utopian quality in some respects, they would also decry the state of sexual servitude the institution of slavery sanctioned and promoted. Though she knows she is violating the bounds of propriety by exposing the truth of such abuses, Child declares that "it is a matter of conscience not to be fastidious." What follows in the tract is a portrait of "the negro woman" who is "unprotected by law or public opinion. She is the property of her master, and her daughters are his property." Child concludes this indictment with a rhetorical reproach: "Those who know human nature would be able to conjecture the unavoidable result, even if it were not betrayed by the amount of mixed population."[31] With increasing vehemence in this declaration, Child holds up to ridicule not only the iniquities of the institution but also the official doctrine that continued to defend the reality of racial separation.

The widely known and beloved writer of children's literature and domestic advice manuals anticipated the storm of criticism her radical treatise would unleash. Indeed, she acknowledges in the preface that "I am fully aware of the unpopularity of the task I have undertaken; but though I *expect* ridicule and censure, I cannot *fear* them."[32] "Ridicule" and "censure" are precisely what followed the publication's release. As has been widely noted, the exclusive Boston Athenaeum revoked her privileges, her book sales declined, and she was forced to resign as editor of her children's magazine, *Juvenile Miscellany*. At least as damaging to her reputation and livelihood as these developments was the fact that her editor and mentor, Harvard professor George Ticknor, not only rejected the work but counseled others to do so as well and "enforced a policy of ostracism against anyone who violated the ban against her."[33] On the other hand, Child became an instant leader and cause célèbre in the world of antislavery politics. A *Unionist* review proclaimed that it was "impossible for any candid mind and unprejudiced person to read this book . . . without becoming a decided Abolitionist."[34] Her abrupt ouster from genteel literary circles positioned Child to dedicate herself to abolitionist activism, one outgrowth of which would be her popularization of the "tragic mulatto" in stories for antislavery giftbooks.

STRATEGIES OF INTERRACIALISM

Child's deployment of the "tragic mulatto" or "quadroon" in the 1840s must be seen, therefore, in the context of all her antislavery efforts, including her editorship of the *National Anti-Slavery Standard* from 1841 to 1843. As Bruce Mills argues, the reform leader set out to "respond artfully to the particular social questions of her day" rather than to "create timeless artifacts."[35] Obviously a nimble writer able to master an array of prose genres, Child's miscegenation fiction represents one more literary mode in which to challenge prevailing discourses of racial and national hierarchies. As editor of the *Standard*, she was opposed to the views of the "New Organization," a group that diverged from the American Anti-Slavery Society in part because the latter favored more direct political engagement in the antislavery cause. Over significant opposition within her own ranks, Child held firm to her belief that the movement should use moral suasion over politics and that the newspaper should temper its message to appeal to the widest possible audience. To Child, the *Standard* was "not intended to meet the wants of ultra abolitionists, but to gain the ear of the people at large."[36]

Like other sentimentalists and Emersonians, she believed that her writing should be directed at exerting moral influence over individuals rather than at making political pronouncements to convert the masses: "[T]he perfection of the *individual* is the sure way to regenerate the *mass*," she wrote. "I am to obey my highest instincts; and in no other way can I possibly do so much to bring discordant social relations into harmony." Child approached her fiction in the same way, which is to say that her subject matter, plot, and characters were devised to appeal to a large readership and to effect in them a moral and spiritual conversion. She averred that "politics and war arise from want of faith in spiritual weapons; both start with the idea that the outward can *compel* the inward." As Child saw it, the purpose of her art, by contrast, was to bring about moral regeneration and a change of consciousness from within, and she was prepared to use every popular literary tool at her disposal to achieve that aim.[37]

Child's 1834 antislavery collection *The Oasis* had included a version of John Gabriel Stedman's "Narrative of Joanna; An Emancipated Slave, of Surinam," an account from the point of view of a British captain stationed in Surinam that presents an early prototype of the exotic, educated, and hapless mulatta slave. Her first rendering of the figure appears in "The Quadroons," an 1842 story published in the *Liberty Bell*, an annual giftbook edited by Maria Weston Chapman that served through midcentury as a fund-raising device for the American Anti-Slavery Society. The plot chronicles the union between Edward, a wealthy white planter, and Rosalie, a beautiful, educated quadroon. After giving birth to a daughter, Xarifa, their sham marriage ends when Edward takes as his legal wife the daughter of a wealthy Georgia politician. Betrayed and grief-stricken, Rosalie dies, leaving Xarifa without protectors. When Edward himself dies of guilt and drink soon thereafter, the orphaned Xarifa finds herself on the public auction stand. Sold to a lascivious master who thwarts her escape attempt by murdering her lover, Xarifa gives herself over to despair, madness, and, finally, death.

The two cruxes in the story—the absence of legal marriage between the races and the failure of Edward to provide for the manumission of the offspring from such a union—are classic elements of the "tragic mulatta" narrative and are manifestly designed to challenge existing laws proscribing miscegenation. As we shall see in the next chapter, William Wells Brown borrowed the same plot from Child, in some cases lifting whole paragraphs. Both writers' works have historically been the subject of sharp critique for exploiting the figure of the passive, ill-fated mulatta slave, whose "tragic" nature is commensurate with how closely she approximates white feminine ideals. Karcher's assessment is illustrative: "Far from encouraging the development of alternative cultural ideals, the archetype of the 'tragic quadroon,' whose tinge of black blood barred her from marrying the white gentleman she loved, implicitly condemned Blacks to pursue the hopelessly elusive goal of becoming white."[38] Here, I want to argue for the importance of distinguishing between the legacy of the mulatta figure in literary history and the precise sociopolitical conditions to which Child was responding in bringing it into representational existence at this particular historical moment. Child's textual strategy regarding the figure was at once politically engaged and highly contrived. In a climate of intense racialism, she was less concerned in her sentimental fiction with prompting "Blacks to pursue" a particular real-world "goal" than she was with offering white middle-class readers—the same readers who authorized and produced such racialism—"parables of transcendence," in Bruce Mills's formulation.[39] In this context, the "transcendence" has less to do with offering the reader triumphantly liberational characters and narratives than with creating the conditions whereby whites might unthreateningly envision *themselves* if not black, then brown. Far from disavowing her characters' blackness, the antislavery reformer makes the radical move of appealing to her audience to embrace such an identification as their own—or at least as an element of their family. That is, an underappreciated aspect of the cultural work of Child's fiction is the extent to which she presents as natural and even desirable exactly the kind of mixed-race families that were the object of such fear and scorn in the racialist environment of the nineteenth century. Her sentimental stories, then, constitute her attempt to intervene in the national debate over whether "the national body was [to be] conceived as a single [white] human body, or whether the miscegenous human bodies were [to be] seen as a microcosm of the national body," as Eva Saks has described the critical issues at stake.[40]

Paradoxically, perhaps, the literary mode Child deploys to accomplish her goals bears little relation to realism, despite critics' tendency to judge her stories on mimetic grounds. Her highly wrought style is particularly striking in the story "Slavery's Pleasant Homes," whose publication in the *Liberty Bell* follows "The Quadroons" by a year. The title itself works as an ironic rejoinder to a genre of proslavery plantation literature that followed the burgeoning abolitionist movement in the 1830s and 1840s. William L. Andrews observes that the nostalgia evident in that tradition for "the heroic days of the past" exemplifies "a deep-seated resistance to change, a conservatism that would become increasingly militant" among southern writers.[41] Thus, at precisely the time when ideas of white racial supremacy were being widely promulgated in science and in fiction, this story wants to show the essential cruelty and violence that flow from racial hierarchies, yet it does so in a markedly stylized, romantic fashion.

The tale begins with the arrival home to Georgia from New Orleans of Frederic Dalcho and his new bride, Marion, "a pretty little waxen plaything, as fragile and as delicate as the white Petunia blossom." Next to be introduced is Marion's "foster-sister" and slave, Rosa, "a young girl, elegantly formed, and beautiful as a velvet carnation. It was a beautiful contrast to see her beside her mistress, like a glittering star in attendance upon the pale and almost vanishing moonsickle."[42] Though our presentist gaze may prompt us to dismiss the exoticism and aestheticization of such passages, these aspects of Child's manner of description merit closer attention. The floral metaphors and florid style, so alien to our literary taste, reflect Child's fascination with Swedenborg's doctrine of "correspondences," in which spiritual truths are revealed in the harmonies of nature. They are also strategically rendered to please her antebellum audience, drawing them into a position of identification with the darker-skinned heroine. In this way, readers are seduced by the familiar images of sentimental fiction into adopting a sympathetic posture toward characters and events that would otherwise prove distressing. Moreover, in a move characteristic of Child's fiction, the juxtaposition of the portraits of the interracial half-sisters serves to temper the element of racial hierarchy, conveying instead a sense of the characters' complementarity and interconnectedness. This sense is intensified in a scene of sororal play when Marion dresses Rosa in her jewels: "'You shall wear my golden ornaments whenever you ask for them,' said she; 'they contrast so well with the soft, brown satin of your neck and arms. I will wear pearls and amethysts; but gold needs the dark complexion to show its richness. Besides, you are a handsome creature, Rosa, and gold is none too good for you.'"[43]

This aestheticization of racial difference, contrived as it may be, nonetheless carries the social import of instilling in readers' imaginations a vision or fantasy of interracial harmony that turns the popular cultural nightmare of "amalgamation" into a pleasant and hopeful daydream for the future.[44] Granted such narrative strategies participate in aspects of romantic racialism, yet Child indisputably endeavors here to unsettle normative patterns of race relations in which, to Saks, "the national body was explicitly conceived as a white body, while blacks were portrayed in a simile as the fraction of polluting blood within this body, an unassimilable *clot* in the national body and the white family."[45] Child transforms this metaphorical "unassimilable clot" within the family into a complementary and salutary whole.

Thus, the primary work of "Slavery's Pleasant Homes" is not only to show the victimization of both white and black families by the slave system but to compel readers to question their notions concerning the racial configuration of the family itself. Besides Marion's and Rosa's status as "foster" sisters, Frederic, the slaveholder, has a favorite slave, George, who happens also to be Frederic's "handsome quadroon brother." The story's cynical title signals to the reader that this scene of ostensible familial bliss will soon be shattered utterly. Indeed, the sexual violence that permeates the story prefigures Harriet Jacobs's *Incidents in the Life of a Slave Girl*, edited by Child and published in 1861.[46]

The conflict begins when George and Rosa, the two slaves, fall in love and "utter the marriage vow to each other, in the silent presence of the stars." When Frederic oversees Rosa's "beaming expression" directed toward George, his proprietary instincts are aroused. He pursues Rosa himself, placing her and Marion in the position of sexual rivals and provoking a scene of interfamilial, interracial shame and brutality: "In the morning, Rosa came to dress [Marion], as usual, but she avoided looking in her face, and kept her eyes fixed on the ground. As she knelt to tie the satin shoe, Marion spoke angrily of her awkwardness, and gave her a blow. It was the first time she had struck her; for they really loved each other." The violence quickly escalates after Rosa, sexually violated by Frederic, dies in premature labor, pregnant with the master's child. In one of her most daring plot turns, Child presents a sympathetic portrayal of George's act of retribution in murdering his brother/master. Once again, the fraternal bond is stressed when George contemplates his act of revenge: " 'He is my brother,' thought he, 'we grew up side by side, children of the same father; but I am his slave. Handsomer, stronger, and more intelligent than he; and yet I am his *slave*. And now he will sell me, because the murdered one will forever come up between us.'"[47] To be sure, Child is making an abolitionist argument, but she is also underscoring the fact that Frederic and George are literally blood brothers. She is telling a story that seldom got told, though it surely happened. Unwilling to allow a fellow slave to be punished for Frederic's murder, George then confesses and is hanged.

From a "parable of transcendence," then, the story devolves into a chronicle of the potential for slavery to transform the power of familial bonds into betrayal and savagery. It ends with purported press accounts of the incident and with the narrator's lament that "not one was found to tell how the slave's young wife had been torn from him by his own brother, and murdered with slow tortures. . . . His very name was left unmentioned; he was only Mr. Dalcho's slave!"[48] Thus, as reported to the public, George loses all familial identity and agency. Here, the author positions as hero the rebellious and murderous slave and then illustrates the brutality of his absolute abjection. For Child, expanding the very definition of family and dramatizing its violent rupture under the corrosive influence of slavery are twin concerns. Indeed, "Slavery's Pleasant Homes" presents the reader with the paradox represented by the author's simultaneous representation of the potential inclusiveness of the family *and* its degradation and corruption. Such a representation engages with the proslavery argument that slaves were part of the extended plantation family only to expose the malevolence that accompanied that status. Moreover, Child's desire to challenge and disrupt conventional configurations of the family unsettles hegemonic notions about the naturalness and fixity of race altogether. Finally, Child images the Southern interracial family as the American family, ineluctably interpenetrated racially and for that reason forever degraded by slavery's inherent depredations. While from a twenty-first-century perspective such an integrationist view may strike some as romantic liberalism, we might grant its revolutionary force in a contemporaneous context.

Child's later career reveals a remarkable consistency with respect to the theme of the interracial American family. While the setting of her 1863 story "Willie Wharton" is the western frontier and her protagonists Plains Indians, the work is useful to examine to the extent that it presages the tension found in *A Romance of the Republic* between her radical advocacy of interracialism and her conformity to prevailing ideologies of U.S. national hegemony. Appearing only two months after Lincoln's Emancipation Proclamation, the narrative can be viewed as an imaginative reworking, in a post–Civil War context, of the issues of racial identity and assimilation first taken up in *Hobomok* and *An Appeal*. Indeed, Child saw parallels between the social ramifications of the large-scale American Indian removals that occurred throughout the West after the Civil War and the problem of how to incorporate newly freed slaves into mainstream society such that they might become productive U.S. citizens. Formally, as well, Child draws parallels between the "tragic mulatta" and the wayward Native American girl who Willie, a six-year-old frontier boy, finds stranded on the prairie. Though not destined for madness or death like her mulatta counterpart, the lost girl possesses the same alluring, wistful exoticism as Child's black characters: "But *such* eyes!" Child writes. "Large and lambent, with a foreshadowing of sadness in their expression. They shone in her dark face like moonlit waters in the dusky landscape of evening."[49]

Willie leads the young Native American girl to the Wharton home, where she is welcomed as though she were a stray pet. The boy's siblings refer to her as a "prairie-puss" and a "pappoose," until Willie responds protectively, "She a'n't a pappoose, she's a little girl . . . and she's *my* little girl. I didn't hunt her; I found her."[50] This proprietary attitude young Willie adopts toward the American Indian wanderer foreshadows their future connubial bond. Throughout the tale, much attention is devoted to the lost girl's hair and dress. She is described as wearing "a mop of black hair, cut in a straight line just above the eyes." Moreover, "her only garment was a short kirtle of plaited grass not long enough to conceal her chubby knees." In the first of several references to her appearance, Willie's older brother, Charley, declares, "Moppet, you'd look pretty, if you wore your hair like folks."[51] In this way, Child maps out the boundaries of difference between Native Americans and the frontier settlers and announces her concern with the issue of cultural incorporation that she attempts to negotiate repeatedly in the narrative. Throughout the story, as we shall see, Charley speaks the voice of assimilation most strongly, reflecting the author's profound ambivalence on the issue.

The following morning, the girl's parents appear to retrieve their daughter, whom they call "Wik-a-nee." The family departs after Willie bestows upon the child a gift of brightly colored Guinea-pea seeds. But the story of Willie and the Native American girl does not end here. Years later, Willie himself gets lost in the woods when he joins his brother and father on a hunting expedition for lost cattle. Twelve years pass with no word of the Wharton's youngest son, during which time the "heartstrings" of Willie's grief-stricken mother have "gradually withered and dried up, under the blighting influence of [her] life-long sorrow." In the obligatory sentimental deathbed scene, Jenny Wharton has a vision of Willie with his childhood friend. Suddenly serene, she looks up to her husband with "eyes full of interior light" and asks: "Don't you see him? Wik-a-nee is with him, and he is weaving a string of Guinea-peas in her hair. He wears an Indian blanket; but they look happy, there where yellow leaves are falling and the bright waters are sparkling."[52]

Of course, the vision describes precisely Willie's circumstances, but it will be another fours years before his brother, still guilt-ridden about losing sight of the boy years ago, sets out to find him. After traveling to Michigan and Canada, he is finally reunited with Willie, who now speaks no English and whose American Indian appearance startles him: "The uncouth costume, and the shaggy hair falling over the forehead, gave Willie such a wild appearance, it was hard for Charles to realize they were brothers." Nonetheless, Charles, as he is now known, returns home with his long-lost brother—but not before he restores Willie's looks to accord with his family's expectations: "Willie's shaggy hair had been cut, and the curtain of dark brown locks being turned aside revealed a well-shaped forehead whiter than his cheeks. He had lost something of the freedom of his motions; for the new garments sat uneasily upon him, and he wore them with an air of constraint."[53] The "constraint" with which Willie—now called William—wears his European dress is a motif that runs through the rest of the narrative, figuring Child's sensitivity to the issues of assimilation and cultural co-optation.

Indeed, at this juncture the story departs from the interracial theme of *Hobomok* to become something approaching a *reverse* captivity narrative. Paradoxically, William finds himself in the subject position of the cultural "other" among his own family. Though not physically confined, he is nonetheless subject to a deliberate program of reacculturation. This positioning of the protagonist as a "cultural captive" of sorts, alienated among his own people, suggests Child's appreciation of the social construction of identity. However, the family is divided as to the proper strategy to bring about his cultural conversion. At one extreme, Uncle George favors a subtle approach, believing that a policy of restraint and acceptance will eventually produce the desired results. On the other extreme, William's siblings and cousins are overt in their disdain for his adopted culture—a disdain that intensifies when William retrieves his wife, the woman the Whartons had known as the young "Wik-a-nee."

At the same time, Child is eager to critique white ignorance of Native American culture and language. For example, we learn that the family had been mistaken about the lost girl's name. "Wik-a-nee," we learn, means "little small thing"; in reality, the name of William's wife is "A-lee-lah." Here, Child's narrative enacts a conflicting impulse between an apparent wish to validate and preserve Native American culture and a coterminous desire to conform to a nationalist imperative of assimilation. This uncertainty is mirrored in the absence of a clear locus of identification in the narrative. As before, however, the pressure the younger family members exert to convince the couple to conform to white standards takes the form of policing American Indian dress and appearance. Thus, as soon as William returns with A-lee-lah, the narrator recounts that "all felt desirous to remove from her eyebrows the mass of straight black hair, which she considered extremely becoming, but which they regarded as a great disfigurement to a really handsome face." William's younger sister, Emma, is the most vocal in her opposition to A-lee-lah's looks: "It [is] not agreeable to have a sister who [is] clothed in a blanket and [wears] her hair like a Shetland pony," she complains. For her part, Bessie, Emma's cousin, concurs that A-lee-lah ought to dress "like folks," echoing brother Charles's childhood assessment. The two women decide to sew a dress like their own and convince William to persuade his wife to wear it. Predictably, A-lee-lah rejects the offering: "[S]he was evidently very uncomfortable in her new habiliments. She often wriggled her shoulders, and her limbs were always getting entangled in the folds of her long, full skirts. She finally rebelled openly, and, with an emphatic 'Me no like,' cast aside the troublesome garments and resumed her blanket."[54]

American assimilationism is thus figured as Victorian fashion. In fact, the narrative action comes to a halt at this point in the story and gives way to an extended treatment of the issue of appearance as a marker of cultural resistance and incorporation. The comedic tone that predominates throughout is intended to gain readers' sympathy for the characters, one assumes, but the note of condescension it conveys serves paradoxically to suggest Child's complicity in the project of cultural co-optation. However, such complicity is complicated by moments in the text when the narrator intervenes, seemingly to champion the couple's adherence to their Native ways. One such moment occurs as William and A-lee-lah seclude themselves in the woods to speak to one another in their unspecified "Indian dialect." The narrator explains that where once William considered A-lee-lah's language "lingo," he now considers it "the only way in which their tongues could move unfettered." What is more, the narrator proclaims: "No utterance of the human soul, whether in the form of language or belief, is 'lingo,' when we stand on the same spiritual plane with the speaker, and thus can rightly understand it."[55] Here, Child's religious and political radicalism combine to challenge the hegemony of Anglo-American cultural conformity. Indeed, the reformer publicly opposed the prevailing U.S. policy of teaching English in Native American schools, arguing instead that schoolbooks should be printed in Native languages first and should include American Indian history and folktales.[56]

Thus, "Willie Wharton" is unmistakably alive to the issue, of central importance to radical reconstructionists, of preserving some measure of cultural identity for disenfranchised groups in the face of the inevitability of acculturation. Yet just as unmistakably, the narrative moves in the direction of assimilationism. Even Uncle George and Aunt Mary, who have, all along, been the most tolerant of William and A-lee-lah's difference, express their wish that the family will "finally succeed in winning them over to our mode of life." Eventually, the Whartons begin to achieve their desired goal through "the magical power of two side-combs ornamented with colored glass," a gift that recalls nothing if not the legendary exchanges of precious tribal land for worthless European trinkets. In fact, the vocabulary Child employs to capture the moment A-lee-lah changes her hairstyle to conform to white standards is particularly telling: "The conquest was complete," the narrator declares. "Henceforth, the large, lambent eyes shone in their moonlight beauty without any overhanging cloud."[57]

Here, then, land is metaphorized as fashion, and the "conquest" of the West is literally imprinted on the body of the Native American. This moment of acquiescence is followed by a quintessential scene of cultural conversion in the Christian marriage of the already-married interracial pair. At the same time, however, Child demonstrates a distinct discomfort with such a wholesale embrace of a corporealized manifest destiny. Following the sartorial focus of the narrative, she offers an extended description of the bride's wedding attire that attempts to achieve a cross-cultural syncretism expressed through fashion: "The bride's dress was a becoming hybrid between English and Indian costumes. Loose trousers of emerald-green merino were fastened with a scarlet cord and tassels above gaiters of yellow beaver-skin thickly embroidered with beads of many colors.... At the waist, it was fastened with a green morocco belt and gilded buckle. The front-hair, now accustomed to being parted, had grown long enough to be becomingly arranged with the jewelled side-combs, which she prized so highly."[58] In other words, in its attention to apparel and appearance, this image embodies Child's wish for a cultural hybridity equivalent to the mixed nature of A-lee-lah's wedding garb. Christopher Castiglia has noted that captivity narratives allow their female protagonists to challenge the binary opposition of white and Native American societies: "[M]oving between cultures, at home in neither yet ultimately constituted from elements of both, the captives articulate 'hybrid' subjectivities that destabilize white culture's fiction of fixed and pure identity. By contradicting their pure and essential 'whiteness' with different epistemologies, captives present a model of how, without imagining oneself free of discursive exchange, one can nevertheless write a new subjectivity, using different grammars of identification."[59] Though A-lee-lah and William are the cultural "captives" of the Anglo-American

Wharton family in this reverse captivity narrative, Child appears to be engaged in a similar project of destabilizing fixed notions of ethnic identity in favor of a superior, heterodox notion of subjectivity. It is a familiar and ambitious endeavor for Child, but one that ultimately fails to sustain itself. Nonetheless, it recurs in the story's final image of the native bride, who has become adept at blending cultural genres: "She always wore skirts shorter than others, and garments too loose to impede freedom of motion. Bonnets were her utter aversion, but she consented to wear a woman's riding hat with a drooping feather."[60]

This spectacle of a desired cross-cultural subjectivity continues into the next generation with the arrival of A-lee-lah's daughter, Jenny, named after William's late mother. The tale ends with a lighthearted description of the child that again rehearses the famous phrase Charles coined in connection with her mother. Quips the narrator: "Uncle Charles says he has no fault to find with [Jenny], for she has her mother's beautiful eyes, and wears her hair 'like folks.'"[61] However, since the trace of the culture of origin of this interracial offspring is visible only in "her mother's beautiful eyes," the reference signifies a return to the biological. The daughter's self-presentation is finally determined by the standards set by "folks"—that is, Anglo-American culture. So while the narrative, like *Hobomok* and Child's antislavery writings, succeeds in its determination to endorse intermarriage, the possibility of preserving cultural difference through time gives way, finally, to prevailing ideologies of American ascendancy. The phrase "like folks," repeated here for comic effect, serves instead to register the degree to which ideologies of U.S. national hegemony are written indelibly on the body of the Native American subject.

ROMANCE AND (RE)UNION IN CHILD'S *REPUBLIC*

In an 1868 letter to Robert Purvis, a founder of the American Anti-Slavery Society, Child discusses her reasons for undertaking what would be her final novel, *A Romance of the Republic*: "In these days of novel-reading, I thought a Romance would take more hold of the public mind, than the most elaborate arguments; and having fought against Slavery, till the monster is *legally* dead, I was desirous to do what I could to undermine Prejudice."[62] As we have seen, the issue of the relative persuasive force of fiction over social commentary is one that Child was preoccupied with throughout her varied writing career. Just two years prior to the 1867 publication of *A Romance of the Republic*, she had released *The Freedmen's Book*, a compendium of essays and poetry extolling the achievements of such black figures as Toussaint L'Ouverture, Frederick Douglass, and Phillis Wheatley. It served as one of the first collections expressly designed to instill racial pride as much as to advance literacy. The antislavery reformer continued after the war to make public her convictions concerning the proper course to pursue to accomplish a successful program of Reconstruction, arguing for black suffrage and the apportionment and sale of Southern planters' land to freedmen.[63]

Yet as we have also witnessed, Child's vision of herself and her writing involved a certain degree of detachment from active politics. Despite her prolific publication record for abolitionist journals, she wrote to Francis Shaw: "I think my writings indicate that I work to the same *end* as organized reformers; only I belong to the group of *sappers* and *miners*, instead of laying rails on the open road."[64] *A Romance of the Republic* again reflects this odd combination of political engagement and romantic distancing. It was written as President Andrew Johnson was steadily reversing himself on Reconstruction issues, capitulating to the Southern planter aristocracy on property and voting rights.[65] In spite of—or, more precisely, in response to—that backdrop, the novel portrays a future social order that is multiracial and egalitarian and thus constitutes Child's most utopian, politically ambitious literary undertaking. *A Romance of the Republic* develops the same theme of interracial marriage earlier undertaken in "The Quadroons" and so many other stories, but along with dramatizing the darkest moral and political implications of such unions, it envisions a post-Emancipation America that embraces them as a positive social force. Writing more than thirty years previously in *An Appeal in Favor of That Class of Americans Called Africans* (1833), Child had declared: "The universal introduction of free labor is the surest way to consolidate the Union, and enable us to live together in harmony and peace. If a history is ever written 'The Decay and Dissolution of the North American Republic,' its author will distinctly trace our downfall to the existence of slavery among us."[66] If "The Decay and Dissolution of the North American Republic" gives a title to Child's antebellum nightmare of the future course of race relations in the young nation, *A Romance of the Republic* represents her imaginative wish fulfillment from a postbellum perspective. At the same time, it betrays an anxiety about the social and political precariousness of the newly reconstituted, multiracial union.

Such anxiety was well founded in a political climate in which Johnson was readily admitting into the Union former Confederate states without demanding reforms for black suffrage or substantive changes to proslavery constitutions; in which such states were instead passing Black Codes designed further to restrict the already circumscribed movements of former slaves; and in which the rate of antiblack violence was escalating sharply even as the president was withdrawing federal troops from the region.[67] Adopting a biblical analogy to convey her suspicions in an 1865 *Liberator* commentary, Child compares the president to a fallen Moses: "We have passed through the Red Sea, and here we are in the Wilderness, with multitudes ready to bow down, and worship the gold calf of trade and a doubtful sort of Moses, who seems to occupy himself more earnestly with striving to save the drowning host of pharaoh than he does with leading Israel into the promised land."[68] *A Romance of the Republic*, then, is designed as a kind of sentimental antidote to the unstable, tenuous nature of the presidential Reconstruction period. Further, to be successful, Child believed, Reconstruction would have to entail both the kind of large-scale constitutional and congressional reforms the term has come to denote and a far more introspective "reconstruction" of individual consciousness on the part of the Republic's citizens. To accomplish the latter, she turned to fiction, just as she had earlier.

Like her early antislavery works, the novel is set in the antebellum South and tells the story of two sisters, Flora and Rosabella, both quadroons. They are the products of a legally unsanctioned union between their father, Alfred Royal, a New Orleans merchant, and a French West Indian slave, now dead. Recalling the plot of "The Quadroons," Royal dies suddenly and in debt, having failed to manumit his daughters, who are unaware of their "true" race until they are threatened with being sold as property by their father's creditors. They are saved from the auction block by Gerald Fitzgerald, a wealthy Georgian slaveholder, who purchases the sisters in secret, enacts a sham marriage with the elder Rosa, and convinces the pair to hide themselves on his Savannah plantation.[69] Soon, Fitzgerald begins to demand sexual favors from Flora as well. Desperate, the younger sister flees to a nearby estate, where she encounters Mrs. Delano, a Boston matron visiting a neighboring plantation who becomes the younger sister's lifelong protector.

As in earlier stories, Child exploits the flourishes of the romance genre such that the central characters are stylized and schematized out of all claim to verisimilitude. For instance, the narrator repeatedly contrasts Flora and Mrs. Delano in terms that echo the earlier pairing in "Slavery's Pleasant Homes": "As they sat thus, they made a beautiful picture. The lady, mature in years, but scarcely showing the touch of time, was almost as fair as an Albiness, with serene lips, and a soft moonlight expression in her eyes. Every attitude and every motion indicated quietude and refinement. The young girl, on the contrary, even when reclining, seemed like impetuosity in repose for a moment, but just ready to spring. Her large dark eyes laughed and flashed and wept by turns, and her warmly tinted face glowed like the sunlight, in its setting of glossy black hair."[70]

Once again, the conventional reading of such a passage is to see in it a racist romanticizing of the exotic "other." Rather, I submit that the focus of the romanticization is not one or the other subject in isolation but the entire scene of contrast *and* complementarity. It is as if Child's characters—black and white— become "beautiful picture[s]," visual and cognitive experiments designed to appeal to genteel readers' sense of aesthetic harmony to advance the sociopolitical goal of integration. Readers today may reject such aestheticization of racial difference, but in the post-Emancipation climate of racial terror, it was a rhetorical tactic Child hoped would have politically persuasive effects.

Child's political optimism has its origins in her adherence to the ideas of Charles Fourier—for Child, Swedenborg's spiritual successor—and his faith in the reconstructability of society. In 1862, she wrote to Ohio congressman William P. Cutler: "My belief is, that when generations of colored people have had a fair chance for education and the acquisition of wealth, the prejudice against them, originating in their degraded position, will pass away, and our moral and intellectual estimate of a man will be no more affected by the color of his skin, than it now is by the color of his hair."[71] In treating skin color, like hair, as an accidental marker of aesthetic difference, Child, in her stories and in *A Romance of the Republic*, is attempting to hasten the arrival of such a future. In other words, nothing could be more self-conscious or politically strategic than Child's narrative aesthetic. The fact that the overpowering thematic analogy in the novel is the resemblance between the characters and the natural world is no accident; Child aimed to underscore the naturalness and

therefore the virtue of racial variation amid a climate of growing interracial antagonism. The following meditation late in the
story on the diverse kinds of beauty to be found in successive
generations of flowers moves directly into a description of Rosa's
daughter, Eulalia: "Nature is very capricious in the varieties she
produces by mixing flowers with each other. Sometimes the different tints of each are blended in a new color; compounded of
both; sometimes the color of one is delicately shaded into the
other; . . . Nature had indulged in one of her freaks in the production of Eulalia, a maiden of fifteen summers, the only surviving child of Mr. and Mrs. King. She inherited her mother's tall,
flexile form, and her long dark eyelashes, eyebrows, and hair;
but she had her father's large blue eyes, and his rose-and-white
complexion."[72]

Such flattering portraits of interracial cross-pollination clearly
work as a rhetorical enticement aimed at a readership steeped in
the new racial science of Anglo-Saxon hegemony and witness to
a new postwar emphasis on racial separation. The most explicit
vision of a multiracial, multiethnic republic appears toward the
conclusion of the narrative, when the second generation speculates about the blossoming affection between half-siblings
Eulalia and Gerald. Flora's husband remarks that "nations and
races have been pretty thoroughly mixed up in the ancestry of
our children. What with African and French, Spanish, American,
and German, I think the dangers of too close relationship are
safely diminished."[73] Here, Child turns on its head the long-
standing association between miscegenation and incest through
a radically revised notion of genetic ancestry that transcends di-
chotomized proportions of black and white "blood," embracing
instead an original and visionary construct of ethnic and racial
inclusion. Child's political boldness here recalls her revolutionary *Appeal*.

As with Child's previous work—and indeed, most sentimental antislavery fiction—the nexus of the novel's dramatic ac-

tion is the family structure and its rupture under the pressure of the slavocracy. What distinguishes Child's writings, however, is that more than simply dramatizing the pain that slave laws inflict on black and white families, they insist on the inseparability of such families to begin with. A precursor to Mark Twain's *Pudd'nhead Wilson* in its plot, the elaborate story line of *A Romance of the Republic* centers on the consequences of switching babies as well as the tension surrounding the uncertainty of the sisters' reunion. After Rosa has his child, Fitzgerald leaves her to marry the wealthy Northern "Lily Bell," who soon gives birth to a son. Rosa, terrified that both she and her baby will be sold, switches the identical-looking half-brothers. She escapes to Italy with the help of family friends, where she launches an unlikely career as an opera singer and marries Alfred King, namesake to the sisters' father and son of his close friend.

The excessive plot twists and coincidences recall contemporaneous Victorian novels, but here the accumulated effect is to prompt the reader to question the possibility of delineating familial parameters at all. In perhaps the most telling such twist, Gerald, the offspring of Rosa and Fitzgerald, having learned the secret of his past, regrets having consented to bribe a steamship captain to carry a certain fugitive back to New Orleans from Boston: "Since I have taken the case home to myself, I have felt that it was mean and wrong to send back fugitives from slavery; but it becomes painful, when I think of the possibility of having helped to send back my own brother,—and one, too, whom I have supplanted in his birthright."[74] Clearly, the antebellum reader is meant to recoil at the thought that the slave system can eventuate in the atrocity represented by one brother literally selling another down the river. As important is the portrayal of Gerald's uncertain identity arising from his disorienting personal history, having been born a slave but raised a Southern aristocrat in the Fitzgerald family. Here, in a moment that exposes his sense of his own socially constructed self, Gerald muses to Alfred King: "This state of things is producing a great change in my views. My prevailing wish now is to obtain an independent position by my own exertions, and thus be free to become familiar with my new self. At present, I feel as if there were two of me, and that one was an imposter."[75] Gerald's sense of "twoness" as a man born into slavery but raised into white gentility challenges the fixity of prevailing racial orthodoxies; indeed, it threatens prevailing notions of whiteness. At the same time, his doubleness underscores the profoundly interracial makeup of the antebellum Southern family. Gerald himself suggests as much when he asks his birth mother, "[O]ught I not consider myself a lucky fellow to have two such mothers?" He then resolves to call them his "Rose-mother" and his "Lily-mother."[76]

Part of the purpose of the novel—and especially the well-worn novelistic plot of depicting the predicament of infants switched at birth—is to reveal the arbitrariness and iniquity of long-standing statutes dictating that slave children must follow the "condition of the mother."[77] Indeed, the phrase is invoked with scorn in virtually every chapter of the novel. More than that, however, the histories of the three generations portrayed in *A Romance of the Republic* dramatize the inextricability of the races one to another and suggest that, paradoxically, the "tragic mulatta" represents at once both America's changeling and its maternal figure; the orphan whose identity is forever contested and, in some sense, potentially anyone's mother. This conception of the mutability of racial identity and the idea that such mutability is itself an indelible fact of American history and identity—ideas so antithetical to preeminent modes of thinking in the nineteenth century—constitute Child's most radical contributions to antislavery literature.

The novel concludes with a tableau that represents the apotheosis of the reformer's vision, an emblem for the multiracial family of the reunited and reconsecrated republic. It features Eulalia and Rosen Blumen, the respective children of Rosa and

Flora, posing triumphantly above the dark-skinned son of Tulee, Rosa's servant: "Under festoons of the American flag, surmounted by the eagle, stood Eulalia, in ribbons of red, white, and blue, with a circle of stars round her head. One hand upheld the shield of the Union, and in the other the scales of Justice were evenly poised. By her side stood Rosen Blumen, holding in one hand a gilded pole surmounted by a liberty-cap, while her other hand rested protectingly on the head of Tulee's Benny, who was kneeling and looking upward in thanksgiving."[78] Before we analyze the clear excesses and limitations revealed in this portrait, let us recall again that the work was published in the same year as the passage of the 1867 Reconstruction Act, which produced a fierce political backlash. As the struggle between Congress and the president deepened and the factions pitting Southerners against radical reconstructionists intensified, it was not at all clear to Northern reformers like Child that the recent gains in civil rights were going to endure or that the Union itself was going to survive intact. Child's fear of the massive social disruptions that characterized the postwar political climate, together with her idiosyncratic conception of the heuristic role of literary production, contributes to the conflicted sentiments of this final image. Meant to advance the project of bringing into being a postwar world of racial harmony, the tableau instead betrays the work's ideological weaknesses. Eulalia and Rosen Blumen are supposed to serve as appealing models for the next generation of interracial egalitarianism and unity. However, the nationalist zeal of the image all but hypostatizes the figures into symbols of patriotic sentimentalism, a hypostatization that only succeeds in reinscribing hierarchies of race even as it glorifies prevailing ideologies of Anglo-American supremacy. Child's hope that *A Romance of the Republic* would act as an inspirational medium in the service of cross-racial social and political reform in the Reconstruction era stood at odds, finally, with a competing impulse to compensate for her anxiety over the future

security of the Union by embracing the hegemonic discourse of
Anglo-American national ascendance.

The implications arising from this conflicted ideological
terrain are suggested in the depiction of the servant's son,
Benny, the dark-skinned boy whose positioning in the tableau is
significant. He "kneel[s], looking upward in thanksgiving," while
the hand of Flora's mixed-race daughter "rest[s] protectingly" on
his head. Not only does the image fail to transcend the color
line, it also enacts a revised version of Southern antebellum
paternalism—with a light-skinned woman's face. The subject
position of the racial "other" is still figured as the kneeling sup-
plicant, is still positioned lowest in the social order, and is still to
be "protected."[79] Nonetheless, Child's tendency uncritically to
adopt the iconography and rhetoric of American national ascendancy, even prior to the Civil War, should not detract from her
significant contributions as one of a select few among her literary peers even to envision a national "family" reconfigured and
enhanced by the incorporation of interracial subjects. She deployed the familiar tropes of sentimental fiction—including the
"tragic mulatta"—toward that didactic purpose, since in her
conception of the genre they comprised the strongest and most
effective rhetorical arsenal at her disposal.

CHAPTER 2

Revising the "Quadroon Narrative" in William Wells Brown's *Clotel*

IN THE PREVIOUS CHAPTER, I traced the layered significations associated with the "tragic mulatta" in the reform literature of Lydia Maria Child and found that her depictions of intermarriage in general and the mulatta figure in particular functioned as a rhetorical device that at once excoriated the workings of the slavocracy, destabilized the naturalness of racial hierarchies, and provided an occasion to envision an egalitarian future of racial reconciliation—a utopian world of racial diversity in which the interracial family could embody the potential for a multiracial nation. At the same time, the contemporaneous drive for national incorporation, unity, and expansionism led the reformer toward an uncritical acceptance and celebration of prevailing dominant culture ideologies of Anglo-American supremacy.

In this chapter, I look at the work of William Wells Brown, next to Frederick Douglass one of the premier antislavery activists of the mid-nineteenth century. Like Child, Brown made extensive use of the "tragic mulatta" character, most notably in the first novel published by an African American, *Clotel; or, The President's Daughter* (1853). Unlike Child, however, Brown used the device not as a means of positing an as yet unrealized multiracial Eden but rather in an effort to unsettle the very categories of identity at work in the construction of founding U.S. ideologies of national origin and identity. Taking Child as a starting point, Brown manipulates the discourses of sentimentalism and reform rhetoric in his use of the mixed-race subject to interrogate contemporary orthodoxies of race and American nationalism at midcentury.[1] In *Doers of the Word*, Carla L. Peterson argues that "in appropriating novelizing techniques African American writers were simply adapting themselves to the economy of the dominant culture in which the novel was fast becoming one of the most popular and lucrative forms of writing" in antebellum America.[2] Similarly, in *Clotel* Brown appropriated the familiar mulatta figure to indict the foundational tenets of American supremacy.

However, before I stress the differences between the two writers' cultural projects, let us first look at some striking narrative similarities. These can be readily seen by juxtaposing sections of Brown's *Clotel* with Child's story "The Quadroons."[3] For example, an early chapter in Brown's novel—entitled "The Quadroon's Home"—opens with a description of the mixed-race heroine's attitude toward her new "marriage" to Horatio Green, "the son of a wealthy gentleman of Richmond": "The tenderness of Clotel's conscience, together with the care her mother had with her and the high value she placed upon virtue, required an outward marriage; though she well knew that a union with her proscribed race was unrecognized by law, and therefore the ceremony would give her no legal hold on Horatio's constancy. But her high poetic nature regarded reality rather than the semblance of things."[4] Compare this passage with its precursor in "The Quadroons," in which Rosalie, the quadroon heroine in that story, expresses strikingly similar sentiments toward her new slave-holding "husband": "The tenderness of Rosalie's conscience required an outward form of marriage; though she well knew that a union with her proscribed race was unrecognized by law, and therefore the ceremony gave her no legal hold on Edward's constancy. But her high, poetic nature regarded the reality rather than the semblance of things."[5]

Thus, the narrative that frames *Clotel*—the sham marriage to a slaveholder, the birth of a daughter, the husband's betrayal and subsequent marriage to a wealthy white woman, his death and the ensuing sale of that daughter on the public auction stand—mirrors Child's earlier tale. Brown himself acknowledges his source at the conclusion of the novel: "To Mrs. Child, of New York, I am indebted for part of a short story." In fact, Brown's "debt" extends far beyond the mere frame of the narrative. Here, for example, is Brown's description of Clotel's light-skinned daughter, Mary: "The iris of her large dark eye had the melting mezzotinto, which remains the last vestige of African ancestry, and gives that plaintive expression, so often observed, and so appropriate to that docile and injured race."[6] Compare the foregoing with Child's earlier portrait of Rosalie's daughter, Xarifa: "The iris of her large, dark eye had the melting mezzotinto outline, which remains the last vestige of African ancestry, and gives that plaintive expression, so often observed, and so appropriate to that docile and injured race."[7]

To spare readers further repetitions of this sort, suffice it to say that the central narrative of *Clotel* constitutes a veritable transcription of Child's original story. However, I raise this point not to comment on the derivative nature of Brown's novel or to question its standing as a foundational work in the canon of nineteenth-century African American literature. On the contrary, probing the various ways in which Brown appropriates *and* diverges from the original version—formally as well as thematically—opens up new possibilities for examining the connections between race and nationalism at midcentury and the representational trope for those contested categories—the "tragic mulatto." In other words, I want to look closely at the significance of Brown's having at once, in essence, stolen Child's story and, at the same time, built upon it a complex overlay of historical material—imaginative and documentary combined—that finally challenges U.S. readers' conceptions of American nationalism itself and the "naturalness" of identity at work at the moment of their nation's very origin. Though Brown's central narrative is imitative of Child's, his text ultimately goes further than hers in engaging in the important cultural work of disrupting received wisdom about racial formations and U.S. nationalism at once.

It is both peculiarly appropriate and highly suggestive for the full title of the first novel published by an African American to be *Clotel; or, The President's Daughter: A Narrative of Slave Life in the United States*. As Brown's biographer William Edward Farrison notes, the author appropriates the long-standing legend of Jefferson's having fathered and later sold slave children "to illustrate the ironical inconsistencies that existed between the theories and the practices of *soi-disant* democratic American slaveholders, of whom the famous author of the Declaration of Independence might be taken . . . as an archetype."[8] Indeed, given the recent scientific findings establishing a genetic descent line from Jefferson to at least some of the progeny of his slave Sally Hemings, the novel would seem to demand greater critical scrutiny and stature than it has thus far enjoyed—perhaps precisely because it relies on the device of the "tragic mulatto."[9] Ann duCille has noted the peculiar absence of attention to *Clotel* in the aftermath of the DNA revelations and has lamented that the work has become "increasingly marginalized within academic circles." She contends that "*Clotel* remains a book in need of both reading and rereadings, an originary, enabling text in want of analysis and deep theorizing—perhaps in want even of a tradition."[10] Of course, *Clotel* can already be said to belong to a tradition of miscegenation fiction, but as we've seen, it is a tradition that has been widely disavowed. Following duCille, in this chapter I aim to elucidate various methods by which *Clotel* did, in fact, function as an "enabling text" through its stylistic and narrative innovations and reworkings of the tradition Brown inherited from Child and others.

Published first in England, the novel was intended on the most instrumental level to "aid in bringing British influence to bear upon American slavery," to cite Brown's own preface.[11] His appeal for British intervention is repeated in the conclusion: "Let British feeling be publicly manifested. Let British sympathy express itself in tender sorrow for the condition of my unhappy race. Let it be understood, unequivocally understood, that no fellowship can be held with slaveholders professing the same common Christianity as yourselves."[12] To what extent such political aims were accomplished is difficult to reconstruct. In the terms of conventional literary history, this foundational African American text produced a troubling legacy by perpetuating the "tragic mulatta" figure that Child popularized and that continued through the literature of the 1950s.[13] Nonetheless, we can trace a different and far more oppositional trajectory permeating the novel's structural and narrative complexities, one that achieves a thoroughgoing critique of American ideology at the same time as it decenters racial hierarchies in a way Child never envisioned.

NARRATIVE CONVENTION
AND UNCONVENTIONALITY

Perhaps one explanation for the persistent critical neglect of Brown's signature fictional work can be ascribed to the fact that it is not, primarily, in the "quadroon" narrative itself, as it was then called, that much of the oppositional cultural work of *Clotel* is performed. That is, anyone looking in *Clotel* for the conventional story of the rise and fall of the hapless quadroon will easily find it. As we've seen in its unsettling likeness to Child's "The Quadroons," *Clotel*'s central plot outline is all too familiar. It traces the story of the marriage of the title character to the white planter Horatio, followed by the birth of their daughter,

Mary. When Horatio leaves Clotel for the wealthy white Gertrude, Clotel is sold to several nefarious owners, while Mary is forced to endure the indignities of her role as Gertrude's maidservant. Finally, Clotel escapes with the help of a fellow servant and travels north, only to return to Richmond, Virginia, in a vain search for her daughter. She has the misfortune, however, of arriving in Richmond in the midst of the Nat Turner rebellion and is promptly arrested. Escaping once more, she is pursued across the Potomac and, rather than submitting herself to the auction stand yet again, jumps heroically to her death.

Except for the fact that Clotel's daughter, Mary, survives and eventually gains her freedom, this sounds like an overwrought version of Child's already-stylized original, in which Clotel's counterpart, Rosalie, dies of melancholy following her beloved Edward's betrayal. Brown offers the expectant reader the familiar, comfortable story line, yet it constitutes only a small portion of Clotel and reappears intermittently. Leaving aside for the moment the ways in which that narrative itself departs significantly from Child's original—though I will return to this point later—much of Brown's novel provides precious little traditional narrative at all.

Rather, the title character's story is constantly interrupted by a complex assortment of seemingly disparate textual elements—a pastiche of short stories, anecdotes, biographical notes, histories, transcriptions of newspaper clippings, billboard announcements, and other such artifacts woven loosely together in a collection one might fairly term protopostmodern. Indeed, such critics as Vernon Loggins have commented that "the great weakness of Clotel is that enough material for a dozen novels is crowded into its two hundred and forty-five pages."[14] I would argue, instead, that it is precisely in the relation between such apparently tangential and extrinsic material and the fictive narrative of Clotel that we can locate and identify Brown's repeated interest in exploring various social permutations that challenge received understandings of the dominant social order.

William Andrews's "The Novelization of Voice in Early African American Narrative" is helpful in understanding Brown's complex manipulation of narrative in *Clotel*. Andrews chronicles the increasingly stylized and restrictive nature of the formal conventions of the ex-slave autobiography and the growing need in the latter half of the nineteenth century for black writers to forge new modes of expression. These modes, he argues, would free writers from a genre that perpetuated white myths about black realities while retaining the elements of authority and authenticity that characterized the ex-slave narrative and that had been so necessary to the abolitionist cause. To Andrews, Brown's novel, along with such other early works as Frederick Douglass's *The Heroic Slave* and Harriet Wilson's *Our Nig*, was among those that answered black writers' needs in its unique capacity successfully to occupy "a special marginal position between authenticatable history on the one hand and unverifiable fiction on the other."[15] It does so not primarily by the conventional means of grounding the fictive claims of the narrating voice in authenticating extratextual documents but by a manipulation of this "natural discourse," as Andrews terms it, in such a way that it is rendered incomplete and unsatisfying without the authoritative intervention of a fictive narrator.[16] Thus, in Brown's text, "[n]arrating becomes the act not just of storytelling but also of mediating between the real and the fictive worlds, each of which needs the commentary of the other if the liminal narrative realm that *Clotel* occupies is to be authorized."[17]

This articulation of the central role of the narrator as a "mediator" between the real and the fictive worlds—one who not merely reflects but *transforms* our sense of both realms through a subtle yet powerful manipulation of various discourses—is vital to our understanding of the interrelated issues of miscegenation and nationality in the text. My aim is to show that a thematic pattern emerges in the fragments of "natural discourse" in the novel and that Brown's method of integrating extratextual material with a fictive story line achieves a thoroughgoing—if unexamined—critique of established social categories. Finally, then, the blurring of the boundaries of fictivity that is so insistent in *Clotel* joins with the project of blurring the boundaries of race and nation, revealed as their own brand of fiction.[18]

Clotel begins with a rather conventional autobiographical account of the author's early persecution, escape, and subsequent oratorical success on the abolitionist lecture circuit. However, the first chapter of the narrative proper, "The Negro Sale," opens with this arresting assertion: "With the growing population of slaves in the Southern States of America, there is a fearful increase of half whites, most of whose fathers are slaveholders, and their mothers slaves. Society does not frown upon the man who sits with his mulatto child upon his knee, whilst its mother stands a slave behind his chair." Brown then introduces an excerpt from a speech to a state legislature delivered by one "John Randolph, a distinguished slaveholder of Virginia, and a prominent statesman," who boasts that " 'the blood of the first American statesmen coursed through the veins of the slave of the South.' " Following this declaration, the narrator's voice resumes: "In all the cities and towns of the slave states, the real Negro, or clear black, does not amount to more than one in every four of the slave population. This fact is, of itself, the best evidence of the degraded and immoral condition of the relation of master and slave in the United States of America."[19]

This opening is the site of various contradictory discursive operations, rhetorically and formally. Taking the rhetorical dimension first, this appeal to abolitionist sympathy is double-edged: on the one hand, the narrator wants to make clear to his mostly white audience the odiousness of the institutionally sanctioned sexual exploitation characteristic of the slave system. In this sense, he is promoting a positive identification with slaves in general and female slaves in particular. At the same time, given

Brown's mostly white audience, the threatening tone behind the "fearful increase in half whites," the white blood "cours[ing] through the veins" of Southern blacks, and the ever greater scarcity of "real negro[s], or clear black[s]" works toward a negative identification, confirming white anxieties about "amalgamation" and insinuating that abolition is necessary to stem the tide.[20]

To be sure, this double-edged narrative strategy is pernicious to the extent that it is complicit with racist theories in circulation at midcentury concerning "Anglo-Saxon" supremacy and the detrimental social consequences of racial intermixing (as outlined in chapter 1). However, these passages also function to introduce the reader to the notion of the instability of racial identities, a theme that will recur in various contexts throughout the text. Equally important to Brown's readership, they place the origin of such racial instability where it belongs, not with the advent of widespread antislavery agitation in the 1830s but with the very founding of the Republic, and before. From his title onward, Brown will insist that from the country's very beginning, American nationalism has its origins not in some mythically pure Anglo-Saxon past but in the messy, complicated realities produced in and perpetuated by the institution of slavery. Thus, while Lydia Maria Child's interest in miscegenation issues is forward looking, envisioning an imaginative futurity that embraces racial diversity, Brown looks backward in *Clotel*, engaged as he is in a project to resituate and revise U.S. myths about its own history that give the lie to the facile social dichotomies associated with the "organic society" of the antebellum South.[21]

We also see in the opening of the novel the first example of the blurring of fictive and "natural" discourse that paradoxically lends authority to the narrator even as the lines between the two discursive modes erode. To begin with, Brown flouts novelistic conventions by beginning his story not with an introduction to any of the major characters but instead by embarking on a sociological excursus on the changing racial makeup of the slave population of the South. However, none of this ostensibly "factual" material is documented, though the narrator makes the choice to attribute, with quotation marks, the source of the declaration concerning "the first American statesmen's blood coursing through the veins" of Southern slaves. Afterward, just as arbitrarily, he returns to the unattributed third person to cite more statistics on racial intermixing. The shifting and illusory nature of the narrative voice only intensifies in the following pages, which include a long quotation on the legal definition of slavery; an extended discussion of the prohibition against marriage under slave law; quotations from religious associations on the issue of slaves' remarriage (despite the legal prohibition) after forced separation from their mates; and a lengthy paean on the moral virtues of the marriage institution. Following these expository meditations is a discussion of the precarious status of mulattas. Because they are "distinguished for their fascinating beauty," the narrator explains, they are exploited as prized sexual commodities, since "amongst the slave population no safeguard is thrown around virtue, and no inducement held out to slave women to be chaste." While I will address below the complex racial and gender politics signified here, I want now to note how effortlessly the narrator switches discursive modes at this point to cite as evidence of the commodification of female slaves an advertisement appearing in a Richmond paper announcing the sale of several bondwomen, comprising "the entire stock of the late John Graves, Esq." This "stock" includes "several mulatto girls of rare personal qualities: two of them very superior. Any gentleman or lady wishing to purchase, can take any of the above slaves on trial for a week, for which no charge will be made." It is only at this point that we are introduced to the novel's main protagonists, for it turns out that "amongst the above slaves to be sold were Currer and her two daughters, Clotel and Althesa; the latter were the girls spoken of in the advertisement as 'very superior.'"[22]

What is striking about this section of the text is the confusing commingling of apparent documentary sources—signaled as such to the reader through the use of quotation marks—and the start of the fictional narrative of Clotel. The result is a sort of cognitive dissonance: we find ourselves in the odd position of believing in the truth of an auction the subjects—or, perhaps, "objects"—of which we know to be fictive. William Andrews addresses the effect Brown's strategy produces on the reader: "Confronting these ambiguities forces the reader into the liminal world of *Clotel*, where fictive and natural discourse dovetail and can easily be made to look the same. Instead of clarifying distinctions between the real and the fictive in his text, the narrator leaves the reader to ponder the bases on which one distinguishes between the real and the fictive in any text."[23]

Hence, the reader experiences a certain literary vertigo in the face of the narrative disjointedness of *Clotel*. Yet this very state of vertigo, or decenteredness, on the reader's part is ironically commensurate with the narrator's increased authority, since his position is vital in mediating between the "real" and the "fictive" realms of the text, neither of which is sufficient without the narrator's shaping influence. In this way, Brown appropriates the "raw" materials of history to accomplish with strategic subtlety various otherwise scandalous rhetorical designs. This textual destabilization, then, ultimately sets the stage for an accompanying destabilization of such "fictive"—or, at least illusory—categories of identity as race, nation, and even gender.

CHALLENGING ANTEBELLUM RACIAL EMBODIMENT

Before proceeding to demonstrate this operation with a discussion of some of the "action" of *Clotel*—though such a term is problematic in this context—I would like first to focus for a moment on the semiotics of the central image of "The Negro Sale," the novel's introductory chapter. As one can readily surmise, the subject in question is the mulatta heroine, Clotel, standing vulnerable and exposed, on display for the masses as a coveted sexual commodity. Repeated relentlessly throughout the novel, the figure appears first in the opening chapter, after we are told of the sale of Currer, Clotel's mother, and Althesa, her younger sister: "The appearance of Clotel on the auction block created a deep sensation amongst the crowd. There she stood, with a complexion as white as most of those who were waiting with a wish to become her purchasers; her features as finely defined as any of her sex of pure Anglo-Saxon; her long wavy hair done up in the neatest manner; her form tall and graceful, and her whole appearance indicating one superior to her position."[24] This scene of the auction stand is iconographic insofar as it appears with insistent regularity not only in *Clotel* but, as one would expect, in much of the antislavery fiction written at midcentury. Moreover, as we have already seen, descriptions of such mixed-race heroines remain strikingly similar from one narrative to the next. The sexually charged nature of these descriptions, which antislavery writers used to their advantage, derives from the invitation to readers to transgress boundaries of both race and class at once, since the women are portrayed as exotic, sexually available, and aristocratic all at once. As I have discussed in relation to Lydia Maria Child's writings, traditional critiques of scenes such as this focus on the mulatta's approximation to white standards of beauty and bearing. Such critiques are apt enough on one level, but they do not offer a sufficiently rigorous assessment of the complex rhetorical functioning of the image or what it quite literally embodies.

To my mind, then, such criticisms show the difference between the dual definitions Hazel Carby offers of the mulatta's cultural work. In Carby's terms, cited in chapter 1, the literary mulatta operates as both "an expression of the relationship between the races" and as a "vehicle for an exploration of the relationship between the races."[25] On the one hand, then, Brown's depiction of the slave auction reflects the egregious abuse of power that such events entailed in the social sphere and, more subtly, works to undermine the racial formations that constitute a precondition for them. In understanding the latter function, it is useful to consider Shirley Samuels's view of the role of sentimentality at the historical moment in question. She asserts that in nineteenth-century America, "sentimentality appears as a national project: in particular, a project about imagining the nation's bodies and the national body."[26] Though a focus on the body, and particularly the gendered body, appears commonplace to a postmodern audience, the cultural and political significance to a contemporaneous audience of Brown's insistence on it should not be underestimated. Just as important is the author's evident concern with making manifest the connections between such representations of the individual body and antebellum readers' conceptions of the national body politic.

Karen Sánchez-Eppler summarizes the legal history of this connection as follows: "The relation of the social and political structures of the 'body politic' to the fleshly specificity of embodied identities has generally been masked behind the constitutional language of abstracted and implicitly bodiless 'persons,' so that, for example, it did not seem absurd for the founding fathers to reckon slaves as 'three-fifths of a person.'" Sánchez-Eppler asserts that from the 1830s until the Civil War, the rhetoric of the converging movements of abolitionism and early feminism "disrupted and unmasked" the assumption of a "metaphorical and fleshless political identity." Thus, she continues, "the development of a political discourse and a concept of personhood that attests to the centrality of the body erupts throughout antebellum culture."[27]

Far from a simple scene of sexual commodification, it is possible to place Brown's deployment of the iconic auction stand scene at the vanguard of such a cultural project of embodiment. Further, while the author's manipulation of mixed-race characters may on a mimetic level serve politically regressive ends, it may also work to reconfigure the antebellum body in both the individual and the national sense. Therefore, when the narrator declares that Clotel's features are as "finely defined as any of her sex of pure Anglo-Saxon," the alert reader is necessarily forced to question the validity of the very category of "pure Anglo-Saxon." Likewise, when the auctioneer entices the audience with the prospect of owning "a Real Albino, fit for a fancy girl for any one," Brown's diction has to undermine his white audience's faith in fixed configurations of black and white bodies.[28]

The chapter entitled "The Escape of Clotel" perhaps offers a clearer illustration of the author's preoccupation with the interrelated issues of embodiment and national identity. It also marks a significant departure from Child's original narrative in detailing the heroine's escape from the lecherous advances of her master through the suggestive device of cross-dressing, which is absent from the earlier story. Though I will return to the implications of this scene of gender play, I want first to point to moments of journalistic reportage presented in the chapter that, in characteristic fashion, interrupt the narrative of *Clotel* (just as I am interrupting my own commentary on it) to interject supposed historical material. Such eruptions of "natural discourse" use historical subjects and events as political satire that effectively challenges the political ideologies those subjects represent.

The focus of the first of these sketches is "Thomas Corwin, a member of the American Congress," a conservative Whig senator from Ohio who, we are told, "is one of the blackest white men in the United States." The account goes on to report that Corwin, while on his way to Congress on board an Ohio River steamer, entered the dining saloon, only to be greeted by the angry departure of "[a] gentleman with his whole party of five ladies." The man demanded to see the captain, who satisfied "the old gent," after some effort, that "Governor Corwin was not a nigger."[29] Corwin, nicknamed "the Ohio plowboy," had briefly been considered for the Whig presidential nomination in 1848 until he offended the antislavery wing of the party with a speech deploring abolitionist activity as a threat to national unity. Pronouncing the Wilmot Proviso a "dangerous question," he condemned the acquisition of any new territory, whether slave or free. Here, then, Brown is taking aim at Corwin's political timidity and demonstrating the absurdity of the position that racial intermixing could be contained within artificially established geographic borders.[30]

Next, *Clotel* offers the reader exhibit B, a purportedly true story involving "the Hon. Daniel Webster" of Massachusetts, who, vacationing in Edgartown, arrived at a hotel and sent a servant to ask the proprietor about accommodations. The "landlord," taking Webster for "*a coloured man*," reacted accordingly: "[H]e promptly declared that there was no room for him and his family, and he could not be accommodated there—at the same time suggesting that he might perhaps find accommodation at some of the huts 'up back,' to which he pointed. . . . It was not until he had been repeatedly assured and made to understand that the said Daniel Webster was a real live senator of the United States, that he perceived his awkward mistake and the distinguished honour which he and his house had been so near missing."[31] Brown may have chosen Webster to lampoon in response to the Massachusetts Whig's pivotal support of the Compromise of 1850, which included the infamous Fugitive Slave Act. Samuel Eliot Morison and Henry Steel Commager have written that Webster's "Seventh of March" speech was crucial to the measure's passage: "[T]he North could never have been induced to swallow a new fugitive slave law, unless Webster held the spoon." At the same time, Webster supported efforts by the American Colonization Society to export the nation's black population to Liberia and elsewhere in Africa.[32] Brown's strategy of interspersing within the narrative purportedly journalistic accounts such as these works to heighten his authorial stature, thus forcing the reader to confront directly the unsettling prospect of racial indeterminacy in some of the nation's leading political figures. The most spectacular and provocative of these reports occurs directly following the story of Senator Webster's ordeal. It is presented as a transcription from "a newspaper in the state of Ohio," though the particulars as to the name and date are not provided. This piece of journalistic satire describes a court proceeding to determine whether a "Thomas West was of *voting colour*, as some had very *constitutional doubts* as to whether his colour was orthodox, and whether his hair was of the official crisp." The satirist derisively recounts how the judges "wisely, gravely, and '*judgmatically*' decided that he should not vote!" The editorialist then proposes an alternative method for future judicial deliberations: "Lest the wisdom of our courts should be circumvented by some such men as might be named, who are so near being born constitutionally that they might be taken for white by sight, I would suggest that our court be invested with *smelling* powers, and that if a man don't exhale the constitutional smell, he shall not vote! This would be an additional security to our liberties."[33] This mocking allusion to establishing the "voting colour" of a man from Ohio through his "constitutional smell" likely refers to the especially capricious manner in which border states like Ohio determined voting rights for free blacks at midcentury. David A. Gerber observes that in such states, "[c]ustom and political expediency helped define the voting opportunities of the light-skinned. While the antebellum courts continued to protect mulatto voting, the attitudes of local election officials varied according to local race relations and political alignments."[34] Also noteworthy is the fact that Brown is writing at the same time as such Northern state legislatures in New York, New Jersey, Pennsylvania, and Connecticut were systematically disenfranchising blacks who had once enjoyed the ballot.[35] Finally, the mock-scientific tone of the purported editorial also parodies the tenor of the new scientific racialism, which influenced the 1850 census to institute a new category for mulattoes while providing no means with which to delineate gradations of color.[36]

The task of unpacking the sedimented layers of fictive and "natural" discourse interwoven in these journalistic interventions is daunting and, perhaps, not entirely necessary. Rather, the salient point to be made is that they are ordered and choreographed such that, taken together, they produce certain specific cumulative effects. Most obviously, such effects have to do with exposing race as a dubious legal and social construction. Going beyond that, however, the persistent references to various hallmarks of American democratic institutions—the juridical and constitutional in the foregoing illustration; the congressional referent in the prior examples—are especially significant. The import of the repeated use of such signifiers is to suggest an inextricability between the individual black bodies the subjects of the accounts are taken for and those same iconographic American institutions. The strong implication, therefore, is that the very concept of Americanness or national identity itself is always already constituted by racial indeterminacy.

ESCAPING GENDER/
GENDERING ESCAPE

Though the connection may seem tenuous, the preceding "historical" accounts do find their way into the narrative of *Clotel* in that they are presented as evidence gathered by William, a fellow slave and Clotel's accomplice, to show that the extent of race prejudice in the North is comparable to that in the South. William takes pity on Clotel and offers to give her the money he has earned as a mechanic to aid in her escape to England. He reminds her that she is "much fairer than many of the white women of the South, and can easily pass for a free white lady." Clotel accepts the offer, but only on the condition that William escape with her. Having previously had her long hair cut short by a jealous mistress, she proposes a plan to pass as a man, telling William: "I will assume the disguise of a gentleman and you that of a servant, and we will take passage on a steamboat and go to Cincinnati, and thence to Canada."[37]

After "Mr. Johnson" encounters some difficulty in Louisville in verifying ownership of "his property," William, the pair successfully arrive in Cincinnati and separate. An extended version of the escape is then detailed in an account "given by a correspondent of one of the Southern newspapers, who happened to be a passenger in the same steamer in which the slaves escaped."[38] Again, the lack of specificity associated with such interventions of "natural discourse" and their placement embedded within a fictive structure place the narrator in the central role of providing the meaning and continuity in this "liminal narrative realm," to invoke Andrews's phrase. Absent the narrator's intervention, neither the "documentary" nor the "fictive" component of the text would be fully authorized or effective as cultural-political work.

It is noteworthy that among the varied pieces of "natural discourse" that surface at this point in the text, Brown omits a historical account of William and Ellen Craft. There is little doubt that their escape, in which Ellen disguised herself as a male slaveholder while her husband posed as her bondman, served as the model for the cross-dressing scene in *Clotel*, especially since Brown himself toured the antislavery circuit with the Crafts in England. According to Benjamin Quarles, "They said little, but Ellen's appearance created an instant sympathy in a white audience."[39] Though *Running a Thousand Miles for Freedom: The Escape of William and Ellen Craft* is not published until 1860, Brown provides a faithful rendering of the events down to such precise particulars as a digression recounting the travails of a white slave girl named Salome and Clotel's disguise as "Mr. Johnson." Yet rather than calling attention to it as an extratextual document, as he does with other sources, Brown weaves the Crafts' story seamlessly into his own tale of Clotel's heroism. The omission may signal that, as with Child's original "quadroon story," the author's interest lies less in its authenticity or historicity than in its imaginative potential to enact a still broader cultural critique. In this instance, then, the "natural discourse" surrounding the story of the Crafts is imaginatively transformed in a significant departure from prior accounts that subtly, but decidedly, unsettles prevailing codes of gender as well as racial identity.

The sheer frequency of scenes of cross-dressing in *Clotel*, together with their increasing elaboration, suggests the importance of the motif to Brown. For example, when the story of Clotel resumes, three chapters after her escape is chronicled, we learn that our heroine adopts her disguise again for the stagecoach ride from Cincinnati back to Richmond, where she hopes to be reunited with Mary, her daughter. Whereas in the first instance all we are told about her costume is that she wears "a neat suit of black" and "a white silk handkerchief" to cover her smooth chin, the second time the description is far more intricate. We are told that for this trip she poses as an "Italian or Spanish gentleman" and that "in addition to the fine suit of black cloth, a splendid pair of dark false whiskers covered the sides of her face, while the curling moustache found its place upon the upper lip."[40]

Moreover, where previously "Mr. Johnson" had shied away from public view as much as possible, "he" participates actively in "his" second appearance when the subject turns to temperance on board the stagecoach. Indeed, so fully does Clotel succeed in passing as a white aristocratic gentleman that she attracts the flirtatious attentions of young women on board. And in a passage of syntactic ambiguity that conveys the intensity with which Brown is engaged in this scene of gender play, the possibility that "Mr. Johnson" returns such advances is left open:

"Clotel and they had not only given their opinions as regarded the merits of the discussion, but that sly glance of the eye, which is ever given where the young of both sexes meet, had been freely at work. The American ladies are rather partial to foreigners, and Clotel had the appearance of a fine Italian."[41] The combined effect of these scenes is to convey the inescapable sense that gender roles may be as mutable and suspect as prevailing categories of racial classifications. Along these lines, Marjorie Garber has argued that "the most extraordinary cultural work done by the transvestite in the context of American 'race-relations' is to foreground the impossibility of taxonomy, the fatal limitation of classification *as* segregation, the inevitability of 'miscegenation' as misnomer."[42]

Brown returns to the motif yet again in a chapter devoted to the escape of Mary, Clotel's daughter. In "The Escape," we are introduced to the character George, who, like Mary and her mother, "could boast that his father was an American statesman." George is a servant in the same house as Mary, and the two dream of freedom and marriage. When the young suitor is arrested and sentenced to death for his participation in the Turner rebellion, however, Mary, echoing her mother, offers to "exchange clothes" with him during a prison visit so that he may "attempt his escape in disguise." George is reluctant to place Mary in jeopardy but finally agrees to the plan after being persuaded that Mary will not "receive any injury" when the ruse is discovered. The narrator remarks that "as George was of small stature and both were white, there was no difficulty in his passing out without detection." With the help of abolitionist farmers in Ohio, George reaches freedom in Canada and later makes his way to England.[43]

Cross-dressing, then, becomes the vehicle for the attainment of freedom in the two instances in the novel that portray successful escapes from slavery. Clotel, as we have seen, also dresses in drag when she returns south in search of her daughter, and I will discuss her unhappy fate shortly. Importantly, it is through her agency alone that William is liberated; she engineers the disguise and commits the deception necessary for the pair to make their escape to the free states. Again in the later episode, it is George's freedom that is secured, but it is Mary whom Brown invests with the stronger subjectivity and the active agency to hatch the plot to switch roles with her beloved. These scenes from *Clotel* constitute important departures from Child's originating narrative in that they dramatize Brown's concern with countering prevailing codes of gender definition. At least until her extraordinarily stylized and iconic demise, Brown's mulatta character is far from "tragic." Although biographical information is scant on Brown's ties to the early movement to advance women's rights, Farrison notes that the author participated in joint speaking engagements with such feminists as Susan B. Anthony and Frances Ellen Watkins Harper. Indeed, although he was never active in the suffrage campaigns of blacks and women, according to Farrison, women's rights constituted "one of the passions" of Brown's life, along with temperance and prison reform.[44]

Intentionally or not, cross-dressing functions as a figure for the interpenetrating discourses of race and gender in *Clotel*, in that George's and Mary's freedom from the confinements of legal constructions of race (or at least from their most egregious manifestations in the United States) is accomplished through the very same mechanism that works to challenge dominant conventions of gender construction. The conjunction of the two discourses through the thematic vehicle of cross-dressing produces the liberational potential figured in the successful escape and subsequent reunion of the light-skinned couple.

"TRAGIC" NATIONALISM

Ultimately, however, Clotel's significance to Brown concerns issues of race and gender only insofar as they overlap with questions of national identity, and here the narrative takes its most "tragic" turn. Clotel reaches Richmond at the height of the white hysteria over the Nat Turner outbreak. Her gender disguise is no match for the invasiveness of the local police, who, in a random search of her inn, find women's apparel in her trunk and arrest her as a fugitive slave. Significantly, the narrator then intrudes to stress that the "negro pen" to which Clotel is transported "stands midway between the capitol at Washington and the President's house."[45]

The reference to the geographic iconography of the heroine is underscored yet again when the narrator laments that Clotel's final—and fatal—attempt at freedom occurs "within plain sight of the President's house and the capitol of the Union, which should be an evidence wherever it should be known, of the unconquerable love of liberty the heart may inherit; as well as a fresh admonition to the slave dealer, of the cruelty and enormity of his crimes." The "admonition" is to the reader as well, of course, who is meant to feel ashamed by the hypocrisy exhibited in the gratuitous suicide of the innocent mother "within plain sight" of such monuments to democratic freedoms. Beyond that, however, the passage functions to associate national identity and history with racial violence and villainy. With pursuers on both sides of the "Long Bridge," Clotel, in a passage so replete with the gestures of sentimental excess as to verge on parody, resolves to jump to her certain death: "She clasped her hands convulsively, and raised them, as she at the same time raised her eyes towards heaven, and begged for that mercy and compassion there, which had been denied her on earth; and then, with a single bound, she vaulted over the railings of the bridge, and sunk for ever beneath the waves of the river!"[46]

More than a rewriting of Child's "The Quadroons," which also ends tragically (though less dramatically so), the most direct comparison of this scene must be to Harriet Beecher Stowe's *Uncle Tom's Cabin*, published in book form only a year earlier. In an important sense, this is Eliza Harris's escape across the Ohio River gone terribly wrong, except that here, the reader's attention is instantly turned not toward the beloved, departed soul but toward her founding progenitor. Immediately after Clotel's jump, the narrator offers the following eulogy: "Thus died Clotel, the daughter of Thomas Jefferson, a president of the United States; a man distinguished as the author of the Declaration of American Independence, and one of the first statesmen of that country."[47] Here, the reader is shocked in the first instance at the sudden death of the novel's heroine, yet equally powerful is the supplemental reminder of the Founding Father's iniquitous paternity. While the former effect is to elicit sympathy for the abolitionist cause, the latter is manifestly more disturbing. It at once implicates one of the most revered heroes of the nation's founding in an appalling and vivid scene of coerced self-destruction and, most disconcerting of all, underscores the direct genetic lineage between the runaway slave and the personification of the best ideals of American national identity. Contrary to prevailing notions of American national mythology held by his white majority audience, "Americanness," or U.S. national identity, Brown thus insists, is interracial—and tragic—from its founding onward.

If the novel were to end here, it would not have advanced much beyond its predecessor—Child's story "The Quadroons"—in which both mother and daughter die in similar melodramatic scenes of heartbreak and thwarted escape attempts, respectively. Instead, Brown's reworking of the "quadroon narrative" more closely resembles the conclusion to *Uncle Tom's Cabin*—though with a crucial distinction. Whereas Stowe explicitly endorses the African colonizationist efforts under way at midcentury in the conclusion of her best seller, Brown's surviving characters, like the author himself, make their way from the United States to the more hospitable political climate of Europe. Mary and George, both described as "offspring of American statesmen," are, after a separation of several years, finally reunited in

Dunkirk, France, where Mary has lived as a widow; George, visiting from London, has remained unmarried. Thus, what becomes in Stowe's novel a capitulation to colonizationist impulses is represented as an explicit protest against U.S. racial persecution in *Clotel*. That the lovers would resume their lives in Europe is a rhetorical strategy directed at a largely British readership and designed to throw into relief the oppressive state of affairs in the couple's homeland: "We can but blush for our country's shame when we recall to mind the fact, that while George and Mary Green, and numbers of other fugitives from American slavery, can receive protection from any of the governments of Europe, they cannot return to their native land without becoming slaves."[48]

The expatriation of Mary and George resonates in Brown's own experience. Since the Fugitive Slave Act had been passed by Congress while Brown was overseas, he found himself among the "numbers of other fugitives" for whom return to the United States meant the possibility of returning to slavery. After months of haggling with his St. Louis owner, British sympathizers finally won Brown's manumission at the cost of $300. In the fall of 1854, he returned, rather reluctantly, from his speaking tour of Europe.[49]

At the conclusion of *Clotel*, Brown allies himself with his British readers against his own homeland, making a direct appeal to them to act on their antislavery sentiments by refusing to engage in commerce with American slaveholders: "[L]et no Christian association be maintained with those who traffic in the blood and bones of those whom God has made of one flesh as yourselves."[50] The concluding image of "the blood and bones" of slaves sharing "one flesh" with Brown's mostly white readers is suggestive in that it underscores the author's participation in the cultural project of embodiment, of insisting on making visible the corporeality and humanity of the commodified slaves and demanding the recognition of their equal worth in God's eyes. More than that, it entails the breakdown of specious racial classifications, metaphorically speaking, and implies that race may be as mutable an identification as national allegiance. Indeed, Brown declares elsewhere that "in this Land, I am regarded as a man. I am in England what I can never be in America while Slavery exists there."[51] In Child's miscegenation fiction, the notion of interracialism becomes conjoined, finally, with a unifying but uncritical nationalism. Here, by contrast, Brown has revised his predecessor's "quadroon narrative" to make national identity contingent upon social justice.

The distinction between how Child and Brown construct nationalism is integral to the differently gendered function of the "tragic mulatta" in the plot of each writer's works. Returning to the final tableau of *A Romance of the Republic*, for example, Child offers a decidedly maternal vision of an interracial Union to come, in which the children of the central mulatta characters are literally wrapped in the flag. Rosa's daughter, readers may recall, wears "ribbons of red, white, and blue" and "a circle of stars round her head." In one hand she grips "the shield of the Union, and in the other the scales of Justice were evenly poised." For her part, Flora's child holds "a gilded pole surmounted by a liberty-cap."[52] Here, it is the mixed-race matrilineal line that will engender the newly regenerated and morally virtuous land of liberty: the "tragic mulatta" as both mother and daughter of the rehabilitated American nation. Brown's *Clotel*, on the other hand, is backward looking and patrilineal. Even the second generation that follows the title's "tragic mulatta" is linked to its male progenitors—to "American statesmen." More profoundly, the narrative drive of the novel is located in the past almost more than it is in the present or the future. Brown's overriding purpose in deploying the "tragic mulatta" emblem is to imprint indelibly in readers' minds the inescapable alliance between American selfhood and racial perfidy, the pernicious mendacity of the nation's founding ideals.

Resistant Cassys in Richard Hildreth's *The Slave* and Harriet Beecher Stowe's *Uncle Tom's Cabin*

IF WILLIAM WELLS BROWN'S *Clotel* demonstrates the need to reassess the work of the literary mulatta in the sentimental tradition, elements of Harriet Beecher Stowe's masterwork reveal comparable complexities. When read through the prism of a neglected predecessor novel, Richard Hildreth's *The Slave; or, Memoirs of Archy Moore* (1836), the portrait of Cassy in *Uncle Tom's Cabin* offers a countervailing narrative to the much more familiar sentimental story of Eliza. A careful study of Hildreth's prior text will broaden traditional understandings of Stowe's conflicted deployment of the light-skinned female slave character and the multivalent literary and historical forces working to reproduce the figure's radical instability. Hildreth's earlier work interrogates both race and nation in ways that anticipate Stowe's multifaceted portrait of the overlooked character of Cassy. What remains underexamined is the anomalous nature of Cassy's positioning as "tragic mulatta," which is emblematic, ultimately, of a larger failure to acknowledge and assess the liberational potential the female mulatta figure embodies— intermittently and ambivalently but nevertheless consistently— in antebellum fiction.

Regardless of the heterogeneous contemporary assessments of the cultural and political effects of *Uncle Tom's Cabin*, the voluminous amount of critical attention the best seller has received in recent years is united in its recognition of the novel's unprecedented influence on the history of Anglo-American and African American literature. Jane Tompkins's declaration that the work is "probably the most influential book ever written by an American" is perhaps the most sweeping such acknowledgment.[1] Yet for all the attention the novel has received among feminists and Americanists, there is little extended discussion of Stowe's relation to the tradition of miscegenation fiction in general and to the role of the "tragic mulatto" in particular. For the most part, the rigorous commitment to mapping Stowe's precise cultural surroundings has failed directly to address a historical development coextensive with such prevailing systems of social division as gender, domesticity, and marketplace capitalism: the increasing attention at midcentury directed at what Eva Saks has termed "the miscegenous body" and the significance of its cultural representations.[2] Since this "miscegenous body" is a product of legislative and juridical developments of the period, it is imperative—before turning to the texts themselves—to focus on the relation of the most important of these events to the literary marketplace that in turn represented and constructed the mixed-race subject.

NUMBERING BY COLORS

There is perhaps no more highly celebrated fact in the history of the production and reception of *Uncle Tom's Cabin* than its connection to the Compromise of 1850, which contained the Fugitive Slave Act. As the author herself famously avers, Congress's approval of the act compelled Stowe to embark on her campaign of serialized antislavery agitation that developed into the runaway best seller of 1852.[3] Much less recognized is the fact that in precisely the same year, the federal census began for the first time to count the number of mulattoes in the population of the United States. Both legislative and federal efforts were intimately linked to questions of racial delineation and demarcation. The innovations changed the census from a simple mechanism for apportionment to a sophisticated method of data gathering in which race was calculated and cataloged as part of a sweeping effort more systematically to hierarchize the races and thereby to reinforce white racial privilege.

In the 1840 census, respondents were asked to count only groupings of whites, free persons of color, and slaves; the revised 1850 version was more methodical, consisting of questions regarding individual slaves, including—for the first time—their "colour." Since these innovations were instituted coterminously with debate in Congress over the Compromise bill, fierce controversy ensued over the purpose of the new schedule. Northerners contended that the new questions were aimed at assessing the increasing "blending" of America, while Southerners suspected they were meant to betray the sexually reprobate nature of Southern plantation life. An early variant even contained questions about the number of children born to female slaves, as well as questions about slaves' "degree of removal from pure white and black races," though the Senate eventually capitulated to proslavery demands and excised such queries from the final form.[4] The definitive slave schedule contained only seven columns, including questions on the names of slave owners, the number of slaves, their ages, their sex, their color, and whether they were "deaf and dumb," blind, insane, or "idiots." The instructions stressed that "the color of all slaves should be noted." In recording the color of free persons, enumerators were to leave the space blank for whites or write in "B" for blacks and "M" for mulattoes. They were instructed that "it is very desirable that these particulars be carefully recorded." Neither free nor slave schedule, however, contained language about *how* to distinguish among gradations of color.[5] Both blackness and whiteness, that is to say, were suddenly a matter of intensified uncertainty and scrutiny.

Thus, as has been established earlier, the implications of racial intermixture became inseparable at midcentury from debates over the future of slavery. That is, the concurrent timing of the census reforms, together with the 1850 compromise and its component Fugitive Slave Act, suggests the degree to which confusion over the delineation and disposition of a new mixed-race American subject embodied national anxieties and sectional tensions about the fundamental racial composition of the burgeoning republic. By what standard were census enumerators racially to demarcate their subjects? How, in practical terms, was the Fugitive Slave Act to be effective in the absence of definitive markers of race? Although the one-drop rule afforded a partial remedy, legislative and juridical discourses nonetheless placed the social category of the mulatto continuously in flux, only to be created and revised anew with each statutory and legal iteration—*despite* policy makers' avowed and concerted attempts to fix racial boundaries rather than complicate them.[6]

Statistics from the census illustrate the shifting nature of this emergent mixed-race subject in geographical terms, especially as it corresponds to slave populations in the South. Relying solely on "the eye of the beholder to recognize a person of mixed ancestry," the survey takers found that the "upper south was the heartland of mulattoness in America," according to Joel Williamson. At the same time, among those mulattoes residing in the lower South, the great majority were slaves. The statistics also show a disproportionately high number of mulatto slaves in the boom areas of the new frontier, including Kentucky, where Stowe visited briefly in 1834. Williamson records that "mulattoness and slavery went together to an astoundingly high degree in those nine Southern states that were last colonized. . . . In making slaves of mulattoes, Kentucky, Tennessee, and Missouri were much closer to Georgia, Mississippi, Alabama, Arkansas,

Florida, and Texas than they were to their mother states to the east." "Where slavery was strongest and getting stronger," Williamson concludes, "it was also becoming whiter." In this way, the notion of the "eye of the beholder" associated the expansion of the slavocracy with mixed-race subjects.[7]

At the same time, the federal and scientific efforts to classify and catalog the growing numbers of slaves and free blacks of mixed-race ancestry coincided with a "new intensity of white racial exclusiveness apparent in the 1850s."[8] This movement toward an increasingly complex racial taxonomy was nowhere more evident than in legal discourse. Escalating a trend that began with bans on intermarriage among the Virginia colonists in 1691, states endorsed increasingly restrictive "descent rules," which held that "those with a certain proportion of Negro 'blood'—usually one-fourth or one-eighth—must be classified as black."[9] Winthrop D. Jordan has observed that such "statutory homogenization of all persons with Negro ancestry" performed certain crucial functions in the psyche of the white antebellum subject: "For the separation of slaves from free men depended on a clear demarcation of the races, and the presence of mulattoes blurred this essential distinction. Accordingly [white colonists and later planters] made every effort to nullify the effects of racial intermixture. By classifying the mulatto as a Negro, [they were] in effect denying that intermixture had occurred at all."[10] As Jordan, Ian Haney Lopez, and others have argued, there is no such thing as preexisting racial categories; legislatures and courts in the ante- and postbellum periods were actively engaged in defining racial identities and hierarchizing them according to privilege or disenfranchisement in U.S. society. For Lopez, "the operation of law does far more than merely legalize race; it defines as well the spectrum of domination and subordination that constitutes race relations."[11] At least since the 1806 case of *Hudgins v. Wright*, which formally established the importance of appearance in defining racial identity, jurisprudence constituted a pivotal realm in which interraciality was scrutinized and controlled.[12] Thus, the first half of the century witnessed a broad effort on legislative and juridical fronts to make an accounting of—and concurrently to construct—a growing population of mulattoes even as states were simultaneously engaged in a systematic denial of their existence. This incongruity exemplifies how, as Saks has noted in another context, "the miscegenous body was caught in flagrante delicto at the intersection of federalist and racial tensions."[13] On the federal and state levels, the body of the interracial subject was insistently and ambiguously produced and effaced, regulated and denied.

The trope of the "tragic mulatto" embodies and dramatizes these profound tensions and paradoxes of race and nation. At the same time as these seemingly contradictory currents were manifesting themselves in the social order, the literary mulatto emerged as a favorite theme of antislavery fiction. The period marks the burgeoning of the tradition of the "tragic mulatta" heroine and its widespread popularity, not only among abolitionist readers but also among free blacks as well as a fairly broad cross section of middle-class white women.[14] As I have discussed, a copious body of criticism has pointed with validity to the ways in which this literature has served to underwrite racist and patriarchal ideological and institutional structures. These studies have argued that white antislavery writers appropriated and exploited light-skinned characters to suit the sentimental conventions and readerly expectations of the day. In both lived experience and in fiction, therefore, the mixed-race body was perpetually refigured, regulated, and neutralized all at once. Still, the fact of the near ubiquitous presence of the mulatto in the literary productions of both black and white reform writers of the time—even as the social order conveyed continual anxiety and ambivalence about the notion of interraciality—suggests a more dynamic interplay than has previously been recognized between authors' tendency to conciliate white prejudices in

their representations of "white" slaves and their coterminous—
though contingent and contradictory—challenge to hegemonic
regimes of national and racial power.

Of course, acknowledging these complexities is not meant
to minimize the presence of racist elements in the tradition of
abolitionist literature and politics. In fact, as Ronald Takaki has
argued, opposing "amalgamation" was the driving force behind
a significant portion of antislavery agitation: "Even Northern
white antislavery was based partly on abhorrence of racial mixing. Many white abolitionists condemned the institution as one
which promoted interracial sexual unions."[15] As many critics
have shown, the conclusion to *Uncle Tom's Cabin* finally participates in the project undertaken in some antislavery circles to
eradicate the interracial subject through colonization.[16] Yet despite its contentious status in literary history as either racist or
assimilationist or both—or perhaps precisely because of it—the
figure of the "tragic mulatta" demands closer scrutiny for the
paradox it literally embodies: the very mixed-race subjects that
official culture was engaged in a concerted campaign to contain
return—sometimes with a vengeance—in this popular and rhetorically complex literary convention.

INTERTEXTUALITY AND *UNCLE TOM'S CABIN*

In his insightful discussion of the profound but troubled influence Stowe's novel exerted on writers of her generation and
those to follow, Robert Stepto characterizes Frederick Douglass's 1853 novella, *The Heroic Slave*, as a "countercomposition"
to *Uncle Tom's Cabin*. In the same vein but with a different gender focus, Harryette Mullen comments: "Certainly Stowe provided an enabling textual model, especially for fledgling writers
struggling to represent the subjectivity of black women; yet another way of looking at the response of black women writers in
the nineteenth century to *Uncle Tom's Cabin* is to notice the dif-

ferent ways their texts '*talk back*' to Stowe's novel."[17] My purpose here is to focus not on the literary successors to Stowe's masterwork but rather to examine significant ways in which *Uncle Tom's Cabin* is itself always already "talking back" to an established tradition of "tragic mulatto" or "quadroon" fiction. That is, the text itself, in important ways, already constitutes "a countercomposition" in this context, since by the time the antislavery sketches that would become *Uncle Tom's Cabin* began to be serialized in the Washington, D.C., *National Era* in June 1851, the tradition was already well established in the work of such white reform writers as Child and Hildreth.[18]

As Eric Sundquist and many other commentators have observed, Stowe's textual sources were wide ranging, from the narratives of ex-slaves Frederick Douglass, Henry Bibb, and Josiah Henson to Theodore Weld's 1839 collection, *American Slavery As It Is*, a compendium of accounts by slaveholders, newspaper stories, advertisements, and other documents.[19] In addition, Stowe herself, in *The Key to Uncle Tom's Cabin*, cites the narratives of William Wells Brown and Lewis Clarke as important influences.[20] However, in terms of its import with respect to issues of interraciality, and more specifically with the representation of Eliza and Cassy—Stowe's most important mixed-race female characters—Hildreth's *The Slave* (1836) is arguably the most significant precursor to *Uncle Tom's Cabin*. This is true not because of any relation of crude imitation or dependence between Hildreth's and Stowe's texts but rather because Hildreth's contribution to the ongoing "antislavery textual conversation" was so vital and original in its presentation of oppositional characters who, through their acts of political transgression, overtly challenge the foundational precepts and premises upon which the slave economy rests: slave/master, black/white, victim/oppressor. Hildreth—writing a generation before *Uncle Tom's Cabin*—offers a narrative that successfully mediates between conventional conceptions of sentimental discourse and a trans-

gressive radical abolitionist voice that simultaneously demonstrates a capitulation to his audience and the possibility for the
cultural rearticulation of the regulatory regimes surrounding
race and racial identity.[21]

The fact that Hildreth's influential and groundbreaking
novel has been so overlooked in much feminist and antislavery
criticism is peculiar given the plethora of recent scholarship devoted to racial identity and embodiment and, in particular, to
the "tragic mulatto" figure.[22] The omission of Hildreth from
studies of the literary mulatta or *Uncle Tom's Cabin* suggests a reluctance to incorporate narratives like *The Slave*, where the
main characters—Cassy, a light-skinned slave, and her mixed-
race husband, Thomas—disrupt commonplace notions of the
"tragic mulatto" trope through their acts of violent resistance to
structures of domination and authority. Acknowledging the
earlier novel's intimate associations with its famous successor
will help to illuminate our understanding of both the latter's
multivalent literary and political trajectories and position Hildreth within the pantheon of foundational antislavery reform
literature featuring—in dynamic, innovative, and productive
ways—characters of mixed-race descent.

HILDRETH'S SENTIMENTALITY
OF AGITATION

As was frequently the case when whites took on the subject
position of an oppressed class for rhetorical and polemical effect,
Hildreth was assumed to be a slave when his novel first appeared. Indeed, *The Slave*'s first-person perspective was typical of
the popular slave narrative genre of the time and so encouraged
this interpretation.[23] To the contrary, his actual background, as
Jean Fagan Yellin records, was decidedly privileged. Trained at
Exeter and Harvard, he no sooner passed the Massachusetts bar
in 1832 than he embarked on a journalistic career, helping to
found the *Boston Daily Atlas*, an outspoken Whig paper. Two

years later, when his health failed, Hildreth sold his interest in the paper and traveled south to Florida to recuperate on a plantation owned by wealthy Virginians. While there, he immersed himself in Alexis de Tocqueville's newly published *Democracy in America*, as well as Gustave de Beaumont's *Marie; or, Slavery in the United States*, a French antislavery novel featuring a title character firmly rooted in the "tragic mulatto" tradition. According to Yellin, Hildreth also acquired firsthand experience of plantation life during his stay, encountering "wealthy and poor white newcomers and their black slaves from South Carolina, North Carolina, Georgia, and Kentucky."[24]

The publication of Hildreth's abolitionist novel, the first of its kind in the United States, coincided with an upsurge in violence directed at antislavery activism in the North as well as the South. Border states like Ohio had begun instituting restrictive "Black Laws" by this time in an effort to conciliate Southern slave states. Such statutory sanctioning of racism gave license to widespread white mob violence.[25] The repressive political climate made publishing Hildreth's work that much more difficult. After several failed attempts with publishers, he finally put up the money to bring out *The Slave* himself, anonymously, in late 1836.[26] Its journalistic reception varied dramatically, according to the politics of the reviewing publications. The *Boston Daily Atlas*, Hildreth's former paper, admonished: "We cannot too much deprecate the publication of such works. We are aware of no purpose which they can answer, save that of sustaining and impelling a dangerous experiment." Likewise, the *Boston Daily Advocate* warned that the book's appearance would produce "more sensation" than the Nat Turner rebellion if it were circulated "south of the Potomac."[27]

Not surprisingly, the abolitionist press embraced the daring political tenor of the novel. William Lloyd Garrison's the *Liberator* published excerpts and commended it as a heartfelt "record of the toils, the trials, the woes unutterable of *A Man*." Copies of

The Slave went on sale at the Boston Anti-Slavery Office. Perhaps most effusive among Hildreth's admirers was Lydia Maria
Child, already a leading reform writer in the 1830s, who sent a
letter to Garrison extolling the novel as "wonderful" and asking
him to publish a review "bestow[ing] upon it hearty, fervent,
overwhelming praise." Child concluded her correspondence
with a poignant tribute: "If I were a man," she declared, "I
should rather be the author of [*The Slave*] than of anything ever
published in America."[28] Here, Child signals the gender constraints that circumscribed her discursive domain even as she
records her sensitivity to the nationalist dimensions of the abolitionist press's enterprise.

Not only did *The Slave* inaugurate the genre of abolitionist
fiction in the United States, it has also been described as "the
first fully developed anti-slavery novel" and "an abolitionist classic second only to *Uncle Tom's Cabin* in its inflammatory effects
on Northern opinion."[29] Indeed, the parallels *and* contrasts between the texts in terms of characters and plot turns are striking. In addition to Cassy, the mixed-race wife of *The Slave*'s title
character, the story also contains the figure of Thomas, who initially appears as pious as Stowe's counterpart. However, the
dark-skinned slave finally rebels against the ideal of Christian
self-sacrifice following the beating death of his wife, Ann, at the
hands of the plantation overseer. In a climactic scene of violent
retribution, Thomas, with Archy's aid, kidnaps the overseer and
murders him ruthlessly. The scene, complete with the overseer's
cries for mercy, is presented as an enactment of every Southern
planter's worst nightmare of slave insurrection, recalling the
sense of collusion and conspiracy that permeates Herman Mel-
ville's *Benito Cereno*. Instead of offering readers Christian sympathy and redemption, as Stowe does, Hildreth confirms their
greatest racial fears. Thus, it is possible to trace a certain radical
sensibility, central to Hildreth's political and imaginative vision,
through to its unstable manifestation in the Cassy of *Uncle*

Tom's Cabin, one of the most unpredictable—and therefore threatening—"tragic mulattoes" in literary history. Such an unstable manifestation signifies the degree to which the mixed-race female character becomes emblematic at midcentury of Stowe's—and, more generally, the culture's—acute anxiety and ambivalence about the nation's intensifying interracial constitution.

To a significant degree, Cassy's tale of violent subjugation and her climactic act of rebellion in Stowe's best seller have their origins in Hildreth's portrayals. According to Richard Yarborough, compared to George Harris, Stowe's Cassy "is a far more dangerous figure, for there was no readily available paradigm for acceptable female heroism that would safely permit her insurgence to stand unqualified by her apparent emotional derangement."[30] Juxtaposing Hildreth's novel alongside Stowe's illuminates the latter's conflicted portrait of Cassy, a character who is often neglected in favor of the more conventionally heroic Eliza. Cassy's own oral history follows the "tragic mulatta" narrative faithfully, but too often, following circular logic, critics have failed generally to focus on it precisely because of the incendiary function she serves in Stowe's work. In other words, readers' narrow presumptions concerning the parameters within which "tragic mulatta" characters and narratives are expected to operate prevent them from devoting needed analytical attention to the pivotal, dynamic role Cassy plays.

Turning first to the representation of the politics of miscegenation in the precursor text, the issue of interraciality initiates and permeates the narrative of *The Slave*. The title character's patrician paternity is the first fact we learn about him. His father, Colonel Charles Moore, "was the head of one of the most considerable and influential families in [eastern Virginia]." In his youth during the American Revolution, Moore had "espoused with zeal the cause of liberty" and had later been "an eloquent advocate and apologist" in the cause of the French Revolution.[31] In this way, white paternity is aligned with national allegiance.

Indeed, early in his life, Archy wonders whether, given his father's devotion to "the rights of man" and the "rights of human nature," he could "possibly have selected a more desirable father." At this point in the narrative, Hildreth shows Archy identifying with his white father over his slave mother, who is "connected with an ignoble and despised race." Here, too, Archy's mother, never named, corresponds to the conventional categories of beauty we have seen associated with the mixed-race "concubine": "The trace of African blood, by which her veins were contaminated, was distinctly visible;—but the tint which it imparted to her complexion only served to give a peculiar richness to the blush that mantled over her cheek. Her long, black hair, which she understood how to arrange with artful simplicity, and the flashing of her dark eyes, which changed their expression with every change of feeling, corresponded exactly to her complexion, and completed a picture which might perhaps be matched in Spain or Italy, but for which, it would be vain to seek a rival among the pale-faced, languid beauties of eastern Virginia."[32]

The attention to detailing the exoticism of the "tint" to Archy's mother's "complexion," her "long, black hair," and the "flashing of her dark eyes"—together with the disparaging comparisons to the anemic qualities of her "languid" white counterparts—is familiar to us from the "tragic mulatto" tradition Child would popularize in the 1840s. However, the context and tone of this particular deployment of the convention are unusual in that the object of this racially eroticized, objectified assessment is not a lover, as is typical, but is instead the hero's mother. Indeed, in an unusually frank reflection for the genre, the narrator is explicit about the incestuous implications involved: "I describe her more like a lover than a son. But in truth, her beauty was so uncommon, as to draw my attention while I was yet a child ;—and many an hour have I watched her, almost

with a lover's earnestness, while she fondled me on her lap, and
tears and smiles chased each other alternately over a face, the expression of which was ever changing, yet always beautiful."[33]

In Eva Saks's formulation, when race is essentialized as a
proportion of "blood," profound anxiety about the appropriate
"family boundaries" results: "The taboo of too different (amal-
gamation/miscegenation) is interchangeable with the taboo of
too similar (incest), since both crimes rely on a pair of bodies
which are mutually constitutive of each other's deviance, a pair
of bodies in which each body is the signifier of the deviance of
the other."[34] Yet Hildreth is not so much interested in the act of
incest in and of itself (which Archy's later romantic liaison with
Cassy undeniably constitutes, since both have the same father) as
he is in exposing the corrupting power structures with which
the two practices become implicated through the corrosive influence of slave-holding patriarchal authority. In one early
passage, for example, Archy hopes to escape the capricious treatment of Colonel Moore's eldest son by invoking Moore's
"paternal tenderness," though Moore has never before acknowledged his true relation to Archy, and Archy has never before
raised the subject: "At first, he did not seem to understand me;
but the moment he began to comprehend my meaning, his face
grew black as a thunder cloud, then became pale, and immediately was suffused with a burning blush, in which shame and
rage were equally commingled."[35]

Here, then, in a striking moment of somatic spectacle,
Colonel Moore reveals on his body a visual rendering of the
very transgressive act his essentialized acculturation will not permit him cognitively to accept. That is, his very corporeal presentation exposes the tenuousness of racial demarcations despite his
avowed resistance to the reality that daily confronts him. As is
common with later exemplars in the genre, Hildreth astutely
identifies "shame" and "rage" as the shared effects—for both

white and black participants—of a social system in which miscegenation and incest so intimately converge, a concern he will
revisit with increasing intensity throughout the narrative.

Indeed, *The Slave* demonstrates an equal awareness of how
"shame" operates in an *intraracial* context with respect to hierarchies founded on differences of color. Thus, the young Archy
identifies with his white father and senses his elevated status as a
light-skinned slave: "At this time, I prided myself upon my
color, as much as any white Virginian of them all; . . . [L]ike my
poor mother, I thought myself of a superior caste, and would
have felt it as a degradation, to put myself on a level with men a
few shades darker than myself."[36] Such depictions of class stratifications among slave populations were a typical component of
antislavery fiction, including *Uncle Tom's Cabin*.[37] The extraordinary feature of Hildreth's early text is that it contains an internal
critique of such colorism. Presented in a heuristic context,
Archy reflects on his transformed attitude after establishing relations with Cassy, who, though a mulatta, is "a few shades darker"
than himself: "Cassy had perhaps more African blood than I; but
this was a point—however weighty and important, I had at first
esteemed it—which, as I became more acquainted with her,
seemed continually of less consequence, and soon disappeared
entirely from my thoughts."[38]

Clearly, Hildreth displays here an interest in discrediting the
intraracial hierarchies of color that such writers as Stowe repro-
duced without serious challenge. Further, it suggests a sensitivity
to and critique of color stratifications not typical of antislavery
writings. This prior text is also more overtly concerned with the
conjunction of interraciality and incest than its famous successor, a concern that reappears in connection with the union of
Archy and Cassy, both offspring of Colonel Moore. This time,
Hildreth focuses on the moral hypocrisies of an institution that
would condemn such a marriage at the same time that it denies
subjects knowledge of their paternity. Here, Archy speculates

about such inequities as he ponders his mistress's acquiescence to the union despite her knowledge of the couple's shared familial bonds: "Whatever she might know, she discovered in it no impediment to my marriage with Cassy. Nor did I;—for how could that same regard for the *decencies of life*—such is the soft phrase which justifies the most unnatural cruelty—that refused to acknowledge our paternity, or to recognize any relationship between us, pretend at the same time, and on the sole ground of relationship, to forbid our union?"[39]

Despite his wife's compassion, the jealous and proprietary Colonel Moore forbids the couple to marry. Nonetheless, they perform a wedding ceremony themselves in his absence. Upon his return, however, Colonel Moore corners Cassy and demands that she accede to his demand to "take her himself." Later, Cassy relates the incident to Archy, explaining that she was spared only by the fortuitous return of Mrs. Moore and her daughter. She ends her account with the desperate declaration, "Oh Archy!—and he my father!"[40] Thus, writing fifteen years before Stowe, Hildreth addresses with startling candor and acuity not only the subject of the sexual exploitations of the slave system but the more complex and interpenetrated issues of miscegenation and incest in a plantation economy. He dramatizes the paradoxical state of affairs in which proportions of blood are quantified and metaphorized as race, only then to be denied in the commission of acts that—if they were recognized for what they were—would flagrantly violate prevailing notions of "natural" and "unnatural."

Such violations of Enlightenment principles of individual sovereignty are also the target of Hildreth's antislavery treatise *Despotism in America*, a play on Tocqueville's recently published *Democracy in America*. Intended to coincide with the appearance of *The Slave*, Hildreth was not able to publish the work until 1840, and then only anonymously. The title itself constitutes a pointed attack on the cherished principles of U.S. national identity, most pointedly to the system that subjugates blacks such that they are statutorily designated as less than fully human subjects and citizens. The fiction and the prose tract work in tandem to inveigh against a power structure that can so totally subvert the eighteenth-century ideal of a reciprocal "social compact": "The relation of master and slave . . . is a relation purely of force and terror. Its only sanction is the power of the Master; . . . It bears no resemblance to any thing like a social compact. Mutual interest, faith, truth, honesty, duty, affection, good will are not included, in any form whatever, under this relation."[41]

This depiction of slavery as a colossal perversion of the social contract predominates in Hildreth's narrative and is often framed in terms of coerced familial miscegenation. It gains intensity in the second volume, which recounts Archy's and Cassy's trials after their failed escape attempt and recapture. While Archy is traded to a succession of dissolute and capricious planters—in the process learning the value of duplicity and tricksterism—Cassy is left to the lascivious designs of Colonel Moore, who sequesters her in a concealed cottage. Desperate to escape his increasingly aggressive advances, Cassy exclaims: "Master,—Father . . . what is it you would have of your own daughter?"[42] Here again, the critique of the prevailing social order that Hildreth decries in *Despotism in America* is presented in terms of the imbricated power relations of incest and miscegenation in the context of plantation life. In these scenes, U.S. national identity becomes indivisible with coercive interracial sex.

Ultimately, the recalcitrant Cassy is sold to an equally predatory Richmond slave trader and winds up in the hands of a slave-holding mistress who resides near the same North Carolina plantation to which Archy is ultimately sold. Paradoxically, it is with the couple's ensuing reunion that the reader is shown the full tyrannical effects of the slave system. When Cassy gives birth to a son, Archy cannot celebrate the event. Instead, he broods over his child's dubious fate and mourns in advance for the suffering his offspring will endure "under the sign of a slave": "That single word, what volumes it does speak! It speaks of chains, of whips and tortures, compulsive labor, hunger and fatigues, and all the miseries our wretched bodies suffer. . . . It speaks of humanity outraged; manhood degraded, the social charities of life, the sacred ties of father, wife and child trampled under foot; of aspirations crushed; of hope extinguished; and the light of knowledge sacrilegiously put out. It speaks of man deprived of all that makes him amiable or makes him noble; stript of his soul and sunk into a beast."[43]

Archy is tormented with images of his child "naked, chained, and bleeding under the lash" and, worst of all, with the prospect that the boy may someday become "that worthless thing,—a slave contented with his fate!" Throughout this portion of the narrative, Hildreth extends the more typical sentimental narrative turn in antislavery fiction, in which maternal bonds and the threat of infanticide are often conjoined. Eventually, Archy is driven to the brink of acting on his violent—though intensely protective—fatherly impulse: "I could not bear it. I started up in a phrensy of passion; I snatched the child from the arms of his mother; and while I loaded him with caresses, I looked about for the means of extinguishing a life, which, as it was an emanation from my existence, seemed destined to be only a prolongation of my misery." Though Archy refrains from carrying out the act after seeing Cassy recoil in panic, he nonetheless remains "convinced that it was better for the boy to die."[44] In this scene, *The Slave* anticipates Cassy's act of infanticide in *Uncle Tom's Cabin*, even as Hildreth intimates a parallel between such an instinct and the dissolution of the proper boundaries between persons that occurs in incest. The source for both violations of personhood, he implies, is comparable.

Here, then, Hildreth illustrates a related principle elucidated in *Despotism in America*: the devolution of society under slavery

to a state of pervasive brutality. "By the confession of its warmest
defenders," Hildreth avers, "slavery is at best but a substitute for
homicide" and "a continuation of the state of war." Moreover, its
introduction into a community "amounts to an eternal protrac-
tion of that calamity, and a universal diffusion of it through the
whole mass of society, and that too, in its most ferocious form."[45]
Thus, this early model in the tradition of sentimental miscegenation fiction goes several steps beyond the usual argument
about the morally corrosive effects of the slave system on whites
by its equation of slavery with racial genocide and in so doing
comprises perhaps the most radical critique of the founding
ideals of the Republic as any published in the antebellum
period. This continual and pernicious "state of war" reaches its
climax later in the novel with the character of Thomas, who initially bears a striking resemblance to Stowe's hero. Like Uncle
Tom, Thomas is dark and physically imposing, but "under the
influence of religion" he becomes "a passive, humble and obedi-
ent slave." When Mr. Martin, the overseer, beats Thomas's wife
to the point of death, however, Thomas abandons his Christian
pacifism for African ritual: "He had secretly returned to the
practice of certain wild rites, which in his early youth, he had
learned from his mother, who had herself been kidnaped from
the coast of Africa, and who had been, as he often told me, zeal-
ously devoted to her country's superstitions."[46] At this point, the
novel takes a decidedly Africanist, antinationalist turn. The
newly rebellious slave takes the lead in kidnapping his and
Archy's overseer, who tries to retrieve the pair as they escape.
Throughout, Thomas's newfound spiritualism is accentuated as
he addresses his dead wife and repeats the phrase, "That man
dies to-night," in incantatory tones. The ensuing murder is described in remarkably stark detail, as Mr. Martin pleads for his
life: " 'No! oh no! Spare me, spare me !—one half hour longer—
I have much—' He did not live to finish the sentence. The gun

flashed; the ball penetrated his brain, and he fell dead without a struggle."[47]

To be sure, the racist ideology inscribed in Thomas's spiritualism, "incantatory tones," and subsequent act of violent revenge is manifest. Nevertheless, in this scene slavery as a perpetual "state of war" is most fully realized, and the corruption of the social compact—the most basic tenet of which must be the preservation of life—is most starkly drawn. Further, Thomas's reprisal is neither glorified nor celebrated; rather, Hildreth represents it as a simple act of survival necessitated by the abuses of power endemic to the prevailing "despotism" in antebellum America. Indeed, we can identify a radical sensibility that extends in *The Slave* from Hildreth's insistence on unmasking the insidious conjunction of miscegenation and incest to the dramatization of homicide as the natural result of master-slave relations. By contrast, Stowe's romantic racialism would seem to make such an explicit portrayal of Africanist revolt and retaliation unpalatable, as would be the rejection of the Christian ideals of sacrifice and pacifism. Nonetheless, the liberatory sensibility and antinationalism that permeate *The Slave* do surface in Stowe's narrative, though they do so provisionally. They are imbued in the Cassy of *Uncle Tom's Cabin*, who, however contingently and ambivalently, manifests more clearly than any other single character the influence Hildreth's antinationalist text exerts on its literary heir.

REBELLION AND CONTAINMENT IN STOWE'S "QUADROON" STORY

In *Uncle Tom's Cabin*, the reader first learns about Cassy's history in a chapter titled "The Quadroon's Story," evoking Child's important 1842 tale, "The Quadroons," discussed earlier. However, Stowe's narrative marks a significant departure from Child's and others in that like Hildreth's Archy, Cassy is granted first-person perspective. Thus, when this "tragic mulatta" narrates her paradigmatic tale of the mixed-race female slave who falls from early innocence and privilege to sexual degradation and despair, the distanced, voiceless portrait of prior renderings is replaced by a new sense of urgency. This extended interlude of first-person narrative is rare both in Stowe and in the sentimental tradition generally, and it sets the stage for a story more in the stark style of Hildreth's brand of antislavery sentimentalism. Indeed, this sense of immediacy is intensified in that Cassy's entire tale is conveyed in dialogue and addressed directly to a suffering Tom. It begins with the conventional childhood of indulgence: "'You see me now,' she said, speaking to Tom very rapidly; 'see what I am! Well, I was brought up in luxury; the first I remember is, playing about, when I was a child, in splendid parlors;— when I was kept dressed up like a doll, and company and visitors used to praise me. . . . I went to a convent, and there I learned music, French and embroidery, and what not.'" Then follows the sudden death of the patriarchal father/slaveholder and the subsequent appearance of a seemingly sincere white suitor, with whom Cassy falls in love: "'I wanted only one thing—I did want him to *marry* me. I thought, if he loved me as he said he did, and if I was what he seemed to think I was, he would be willing to marry me and set me free. But he convinced me that it would be impossible; and he told me that, if we were only faithful to each other, it was marriage before God.'" After the birth of two children, Henry and Little Elise, a nefarious cousin enters the scene, who, following the generic formula, introduces Cassy's owner/lover to a wealthy white woman and finally convinces him to sell Cassy to pay off his gambling debts: "'Then *he* came, the cursed wretch! He came to take possession. He told me that he had bought me and my children; and he showed me the papers. I cursed him before God, and told him I'd die sooner than live with him.'"[48] Despite her frantic efforts to prevent it, Cassy's children are soon sold.

It is only at this juncture that Cassy's story departs from the conventional passivity of the "tragic mulatta" narrative, for, rather than retreating into madness and death, as is typical, Cassy strikes back: " 'It seemed to me something in my head snapped, at that moment. I felt dizzy and furious. I remember seeing a great sharp bowie-knife on the table; I remember something about catching it, and flying upon him; and then all grew dark, and I didn't know any more—not for days and days.' "[49] Indeed, Cassy's reaction can be seen as a transformation of the conventional internalized and self-destructive "madness" of the literary mulatta in that in this instance, the "something" that "snapped" in Cassy's head provokes an outward-directed act of impulsive and dangerous resistance. This scene sets the stage for Cassy's ultimate act of defiance against the system that has paradoxically both robbed her of her children and made it possible for her to contemplate infanticide. Her decision to kill her next child to prevent him from enduring the cruelties of slavery places her character in an even more problematic relationship with the very tradition that produced it. Moreover, it can be argued that Cassy's infanticide constitutes a profoundly revolutionary political act of resistance since, in addition to the moral challenge it poses to the slave system, in destroying her progeny Cassy destroys valuable capital. Here, Stowe's character surpasses the seditious rage of Hildreth's Archy in successfully carrying out the same violent deed that her literary predecessor could not bring himself to execute: " 'O, that child!—how I loved it! How just like my poor Henry the little thing looked! But I had made up my mind,—yes, I had. I would never again let a child live to grow up! I took the little fellow in my arms, when he was two weeks old, and kissed him, and cried over him; and then I gave him laudanum, and held him close to my bosom, while he slept to death.' "[50]

To be sure, Stowe intends the reader to interpret Cassy's violent act as the most extreme manifestation possible of the

corruption of the maternal ethic that chattel slavery, by definition, necessitates, and in this, the parallels with Hildreth's novel
are clear. The act represents one step beyond the incident recounted earlier in Stowe's work by the slave trader Haley, in
which a mother on board a slave vessel "jest turn[ed] around,
and pitche[d] head first, young un and all, into the river,—went
down plump, and never ris."[51] In fact, it is around this central
principle of maternal virtue that the light-skinned characters
Cassy and Eliza seem to contrast most sharply. Though we are
meant to empathize with Cassy's desperate act of infanticide, we
are also encouraged to see her as "fallen" in the commission of
it, until Tom intervenes to renew her faith with "hymns and passages of Holy Writ."[52]

However, despite the apparent differences between the
mixed-race female characters, the description of Eliza when she
is first introduced to the reader as little Harry's mother resembles the later sketch of Cassy and places Eliza squarely within
the conventions of sexualization and objectification characteristic of the "tragic mulatta" figure: "There was the same rich, full,
dark eye, with its long lashes; the same ripples of silky black hair.
The brown of her complexion gave way on the cheek to a per-
ceptible flush, which deepened as she saw the gaze of the strange
man fixed upon her in bold and undisguised admiration."[53] In
fact, the similarities extend beyond the superficial. That is, if
Cassy enacts one extreme of behavior on the axis of maternal
devotion—one whose ethical dimensions are ambiguous for
Stowe—Eliza enacts another, more assimilable version. Indeed,
in an early chapter entitled "The Mother," the narrator describes
Eliza's maternal zeal as so intense that when two of her infants
die, she "mourned with a grief so intense as to call for gentle re-
monstrances from her mistress, who sought, with maternal anxiety, to direct her naturally passionate feelings within the bounds
of reason and religion."[54] The fact that Eliza's mother-love
threatens to transgress the limits of "reason and religion" sug-

gests that underneath the more sanctioned form of maternal expression mobilized by Eliza lies an extremity of feeling similar in degree to Cassy's.[55] At the same time, the intensity connected with representations of Eliza's motherhood conveys a palpable undercurrent of identification between the two mixed-race characters. It is almost as if Cassy is what Eliza would have become if her dramatic escape had failed and she had endured the same degradations as Cassy.

On another level, however, these two figures are indeed bifurcated. A fundamental and pivotal disparity exists in the way Stowe presents the subjectivities of Cassy and Eliza: for example, Cassy's is the only voice the reader is permitted to hear, and her recitation of her own story—which extends through an entire chapter—is of profound importance in connection with her role as the novel's primary political agitator. Harryette Mullen argues that nineteenth-century black women writers "struggled in their texts to reconcile an oral tradition of resistance with a literary tradition of submission." We can see a version of this problematic working itself out in Stowe's text through the divergent representations of Eliza and Cassy. Whereas Eliza more closely follows the literary blueprint set forth for the representation of a quadroon slave, Cassy's capacity for violence and incendiary speech places her outside conventional literary parameters. Mullen further asserts that "to the degree that undisguised coercion permeated [slave women's] lives and invaded the interior of their bodies, such women stood outside the ideological constructions of the dominant race and class." Thus, to the extent that a figure such as Cassy "endured much worse in slavery, the fear of public humiliation cannot threaten her into silence." Applying the term "resistant orality" to Cassy's speech is admittedly complicated, given Stowe's white, colonizationist subject position. Indeed, Mullen argues that Stowe "refuses to construct a complex subjectivity for the black woman."[56] My objective here is to employ the term in a limited way to mark a countercurrent in the text that is contingent—but nonetheless consequential—in presenting an alternative representation of the mulatta heroine. Mullen fails to address the "complex subjectivity" that is undeniably afforded Cassy at this juncture in the narrative. Therefore, whether deliberate or not, Stowe's rendering of Cassy's speech as "a textual representation of resistant orality" is at work from the mulatta's first appearance in the text, so that her very articulation constitutes her agency.

Our initial glimpse of Cassy, in fact, is presented as a consequence of her verbal insolence to Simon Legree. As we learn in a succeeding chapter, Cassy is relegated to "field service" after she protests Legree's lascivious designs on her younger counterpart, Emmeline. Resentful of Cassy's station as house servant and surprised to see her relegated to their company, the field hands taunt the newcomer, who responds with an "expression of angry scorn, as if she heard nothing." The reader's apprehension of Cassy as apart from and more powerful than her peers is reinforced when the driver challenges her for replacing in Tom's basket the quantity of cotton he had deposited in the basket of the ailing Lucy: "A glance like sheet-lightening suddenly flashed from those black eyes; and, facing about, with quivering lip and dilated nostrils, she drew herself up, and fixed a glance, blazing with rage and scorn, on the driver. 'Dog,' she said, 'touch *me*, if you dare! I've power enough, yet, to have you torn by the dogs, burnt alive, cut to inches! I've only to say the word!' 'What the devil you here for, den?' said the man, evidently cowed, and sullenly retreating a step or two. 'Didn't mean no harm, Misse Cassy!' 'Keep your distance, then!' said the woman." When the workday is finished, Cassy delivers her basket to Legree with a "haughty, negligent air" as she mutters "something in French": "What it was, no one knew; but Legree's face became perfectly demoniacal in its expression, as she spoke; he half raised his hand, as if to strike,—a gesture which she regarded with fierce disdain, as she turned and walked away."[57]

Such scenes are reminiscent of Frederick Douglass's vanquishing of the "negro-breaker" and "slave driver" Covey in his *Narrative*, though Douglass reproduces patriarchal ideologies when he describes this "turning-point" in his career as a slave as reviving his sense of "manhood." By contrast, Cassy's verbal act of resistance furthers the narrative development of a black female subjectivity.[58] Indeed, Cassy's hold over Legree is intimately connected with her powers of speech. Furthermore, such repeated acts of "resistant orality," as we shall discover, are underwritten by a fusion of cross-cultural influences, themselves crucially dependent on oral transmission. In "Relic, Fetish, Femmage: The Aesthetics of Sentiment in the Work of Stowe," Lynn Wardley has noted Stowe's reliance on "the uncanny power of Victorian material culture to elicit emotion, provoke somatic response, bewitch, heal, or avenge wrong." To Wardley, this "bourgeois sentimentalism" empowers such ordinary possessions as old shoes, worn clothing, portraits, and cut hair and is linked with "the Pan-African religions of the antebellum South" as much as with "the Catholic faith in the power of relics."[59] Wardley's discussion of this cultural syncretism centers on the character of Dinah; yet Cassy seems to be the only figure who is not only able to exploit these various cultural sources of spiritual animism but simultaneously to parody them through sheer verbal agility.

From the first we see of Cassy, she is aligned with the uncanny and the mystical. In the field, "she seemed to work by magic"; Sambo and Quimbo confirm to Legree that she "picks like de debil and all his angels"; tending to Tom's wounds, she is described as "familiar with the many healing arts"; and, despairing over Emmeline's futile act of bringing her Bible "to hell with her," Cassy "laughed a wild and doleful laugh, that rung, with a strange, supernatural sound, through the old ruined shed."[60] Like no other character, Cassy understands the importance of language in negotiating the structures of power around her. Accordingly, she exploits her diabolical image to the fullest, especially in her exchanges with the baleful Legree: "'Simon Legree, take care!' said the woman, with a sharp flash of her eye, a glance so wild and insane in its light as to be almost appalling. 'You're afraid of me, Simon,' she said, deliberately; 'and you've reason to be! But be careful, for I've got the devil in me!' The last words she whispered in a hissing tone, close to his ear. 'Get out! I believe, to my soul, you have!' said Legree, pushing her from him and looking uncomfortably at her."[61] There is an undeniable element of artful self-fashioning in Cassy's self-presentation here. That is, the very act of announcing one's possession by "the devil," especially to someone known for his vulnerability to superstition, suggests a measure of psychic distance and irony that is only heightened by the "hissing tone" in which the declaration is delivered. Cassy's "madness," Stowe seems to suggest, is a strategic and politically formidable device. Here, Cassy's warning appears both to propel and find confirmation in the events that directly follow, in which Sambo presents Legree with the lock of hair (the "witch thing") that contains for Legree such uncanny and portentous significations. Thus, in such acts of performative resistance the mulatta heroine of this portion of *Uncle Tom's Cabin* takes advantage of the convergence of cultural practices that invests with special powers such quotidian keepsakes as the "long, shining curl of fair hair,—hair which, like a living thing, twined itself around Legree's fingers."[62]

The association of this scene with African fetish survivals recalls the character of Thomas in *The Slave*, who rebels against his Christian teachings after the murder of his wife and turns instead to the "wild rites" his mother had imported from "the coast of Africa." In both works, then, rebellion seems to entail the recovery and deployment of the art of conjure. It also intimates a rejection of Americanness in favor of a return to a mythicized African ancestry. In the chapter of Stowe's novel titled "The Stratagem," this confluence of "occult and domestic

practices," to use Wardley's phrase, takes on even greater complexity. This chapter dramatizes Cassy's newfound determination
"to make use of the superstitious excitability, which was so great
in Legree, for the purpose of her liberation, and that of her fel-
low-sufferer," Emmeline.[63] From this point forward in the narrative, the cross-cultural infusions Cassy appropriates "for the
purpose of her liberation" include the tradition of the gothic
horror story. She literally installs herself as the madwoman in the
"garret" and becomes the means by which "[a] superstitious
creeping horror seemed to fill the house." Indeed, Legree comes
to dread Cassy's "strong female influence," which "had become
more harassing and decided, since partial insanity had given a
strange, weird, unsettled cast to all her words and language."[64]
Here, in a scene of parodic dimensions, Stowe confers on her
mulatta character the "insanity" obligatory to all gothic mad-
women. At the same time, it is impossible to mistake the politically threatening force associated with Cassy's oral facility. This
burlesquing of the gothic genre reaches its zenith when Legree
picks up a volume Cassy has deliberately left lying on the table
for him: "It was one of those collections of stories of bloody
murders, ghostly legends, and supernatural visitations, which,
coarsely got up and illustrated, have a strong fascination for one
who once begins to read them."[65]

Such comedic flare, Stowe perhaps imagined, would temper
the explicit threat associated with this episode of slave revolt.
After recounting the tale of Tom's heroic death, the narrator
returns to Cassy's story in the chapter "An Authentic Ghost
Story," which enacts a farcical version of "ghostly legends" and
"supernatural visitations"—but with serious intentions. Cassy
directs herself in a dramatic rendering of a Hamlet-inspired
haunting as an instrument of political resistance. In the chapter's
early scenes, Stowe herself mocks the heterodox nature of the
cultural sources at work when the narrator notes the slave population's alienated relation to the literary stock image of "the

tall figure in a white sheet": "The poor souls were not versed in
ancient history, and did not know that Shakespeare had authen-
ticated this costume. . . . And, therefore, their all hitting upon this
is a striking fact in pneumatology, which we recommend to the
attention of the spiritual media generally."[66] Despite this satiric
tone, Cassy's ghost story functions an act of political theater that
eventuates in her freedom. The night after Tom's death, Legree
awakens in an alcoholic daze to the mulatta hovering over his
bed, taunting him with what he is convinced is "his mother's
shroud": "By a singular coincidence, on the very night that this
vision appeared to Legree, the house-door was found open in
the morning, and some of the negroes had seen two white figures gliding down the avenue towards the high-road."[67]

In this way, Cassy is presented as the sole black figure in
Uncle Tom's Cabin whose storytelling becomes a vehicle for direct action, an operation Stowe at least provisionally endorses in
this episode. Stowe's "tragic mulatta" thus resonates in these
scenes with the radical narrative voice and the extreme antinationalism reflected in the mixed-race Cassy of Hildreth's
predecessor novel. Addressing the issue of the political effects of
sentimentalism in Stowe's novel, Wardley argues that "the aesthetics of sentiment survives in Stowe's fiction as a stratagem for
redressing the asymmetries of cultural power."[68] One might extend this observation to suggest a necessary connection between
an emancipatory politics and the syncretism of cultural forms
that are mobilized in this portion of Stowe's masterwork.

AMALGAMATION, ANXIETY,
AND ANTINATIONALISM

Despite the symbolic import and cultural work these chapters perform, the oppositional potential that culminates in "An
Authentic Ghost Story" is not sustained in the remainder of the
narrative in either formal or thematic terms. Indeed, the pedes-
trian title of the following chapter, "Results," sets the stage for

the political retreat that characterizes the text's denouement, which combines a contrived melodrama of Christian evangelical conversion with a capitulation to the colonizationist politics practiced by Lyman Beecher.[69] In the space of the few pages it requires to effect the unlikely reunion of Cassy with her estranged family, the mulatta heroine is transformed from a rebellious, dynamic agent of emancipation to a voiceless, passive vessel for Christian instruction: "Eliza's steady, consistent piety, regulated by the constant reading of the sacred word, made her a proper guide for the shattered and wearied mind of her mother. Cassy yielded at once, and with her whole soul, to every good influence, and became a devout and tender Christian."[70] More than any other character, then, Cassy is represented as acting in extremes. She metamorphoses with striking alacrity from the heretical, vengeful victim of the sexual servitude of slavery to the pious, compliant mother whose subjectivity all but disappears in the service of the narrative drive toward repatriation.

This instability in Cassy's figuration cannot be satisfactorily explained in terms solely of a conversion experience that accompanies Tom's death, especially since the culmination of her rebellious plot occurs after that event. Rather, such pronounced vacillations in the representation of Cassy's character suggests Stowe's awareness of—and ambivalence toward—the ideological challenge posed by the active agency of the mulatta heroine. Precisely because of her gender and her history, Cassy functions as both the most threatening exemplar in *Uncle Tom's Cabin* of the fact of miscegenation and as the most militant vehicle against its continued reproduction. Thus, Stowe's fictional containment of the mulatta figure's subversive potential mirrors the growing national anxiety over the ongoing proliferation and production of the interracial subject and the need, therefore, for regulation. The specter of a sexually and politically potent Cassy is effectively tamed in her transformation to a Christianized, domesticated mother. Ultimately, of course, the mixed-race status

of the entire family is elided in George Harris's identification
with "the oppressed, enslaved African race."[71] More than that,
the family's exit to Liberia, as Gillian Brown has remarked, allows Stowe finally to "do away with blackness, the mark of incongruity and exogamy."[72] More generously, perhaps, the exodus
also suggests that Stowe could not envision an integrated nation
after the political rupture of slavery, leaving the dream of a
united post-Emancipation republic forever unattainable.[73]

The radical sensibility that Cassy's narrative shares with *The
Slave* thus gives way under the pressure of Stowe's romantic
racialist vision of a Christianized and colonialist Africa. Hildreth's novel, like Stowe's, concludes with a successful escape.
Archy, having separated from Thomas for fear of recapture,
makes his way first to New York and then to Boston, where he
passes himself off as a sailor on board a ship bound for Bor-
deaux. However, it is instructive to note the differences in the
texts' conclusions, which possess vastly different implications
with respect to their authors' views of family and nation under
the slavocracy. The most striking such difference is the stress
placed on familial separation, rather than reunion, in Hildreth's
work. Archy attains his freedom after having been sold to pay off
his master's creditors. Soon afterward, he hires "an agent" to
search for his family while he takes up the life of a sailor. Rather
than producing a fortunate outcome, however, the two-year
search turns up neither wife nor son. In this way, Stowe's predecessor dramatizes the effects for the hero of the commonplace
occurrence of familial loss under slavery over the fantasy of familial restoration: "The curse of tyranny is indeed multifold; nay,
infinite!—It blasted me across the broad Atlantic; and when I
thought of Cassy and my boy, I shrunk and trembled as if again
the irons were upon me, and the bloody lash cracking about my
head!—Almighty God! why hast thou created beings capable of
so much misery!"[74]

Here, as with the second-generation characters in *Clotel*,

"freedom" requires exile from family and nation. Indeed, unable to return to his homeland, Archy remains literally at sea for a period of years following his escape. Having "chosen the ocean for [his] country," he roams the globe, voyaging from Europe to "the Persian deserts" and from there to "the flowery forests of Brazil." His racial liminality becomes mirrored in his geographical liminality. All the time, he compares the condition of the slaves in these countries to their situation in his native land: "It is in the United States alone, that country so apt to claim a monopoly of freedom, that the spirit of tyranny still soars boldly triumphant, and disdains even the most distant thought of limitation. Here alone, of all the world beside, oppression riots unchecked by fear of God or sympathy for man."[75]

Thus, *The Slave; or, Memoirs of Archy Moore*, the first American antislavery novel, concludes with a sharp invective against the United States and a challenge to U.S. nationalism itself.[76] In contrast to Stowe's appeal for sympathy and her abstract Christian millennialism, Hildreth's message of militant opposition must have alarmed all but the most ardent abolitionists. Nonetheless, it finds a voice—provisional, yet powerful—in the unlikely figure of Cassy in *Uncle Tom's Cabin*, who, ironically, has by conventional standards been considered the most "tragic" of the novel's mulattoes.

CHAPTER 4

Public Poor Relief and National Belonging in Harriet Wilson's *Our Nig*

IN THE PREVIOUS CHAPTER, I argued in connection with Hildreth's *The Slave* and Stowe's *Uncle Tom's Cabin* that far from its conventional image of victimized passivity, the "tragic mulatto" figure can function as a serious challenge to the prevailing social order. Nowhere is this more true than in Harriet Wilson's 1859 novel, *Our Nig; or, Sketches from the Life of a Free Black in a Two-Story White House, North, Showing That Slavery's Shadows Fall Even There.* While from her first appearance it becomes clear that the character of Frado is firmly rooted in the "tragic" tradition, in many ways she also extends and counters the convention from which she emerges. Wilson achieves this result by dint of the political ambitiousness of what first appears to be a rather simple tale. On the contrary, *Our Nig* is the first "tragic mulatta" narrative to be explicitly concerned with issues of class as they impinge upon race politics. More than that, the novel subtly, yet decidedly, advances an allegorical brief for economic and racial equity in an emerging interracial nation.

Indeed, by the 1830s comparisons were routinely being made in the rhetoric of the emerging labor movement between the status of the Northern worker and the Southern slave. By 1859, when *Our Nig* was published, Northern abolitionists were embroiled in a heated controversy over the parallels that could be drawn between the wage system and slavery. According to Eric Foner, "whereas labor leaders tended to see abolition as a diversion from the grievances of Northern labor, and slavery as simply one example of more pervasive problems in American life, abolitionists considered the labor issue as artificial or secondary."[1] Although *Our Nig* doesn't thematize aspects of the ascendant wage system directly, it depicts in graphic detail the disastrous social consequences for those who, like Mag, the mother, and Frado, the daughter, pay the price of the attendant "erosion of respect for labor, the loss of independence by the craftsman, and the emergence of 'European' social conditions and class stratification in republican America."[2] Following a discussion of the correspondences between Frado's experience and the historical administration of poor relief, I will move to a reading of the novel in which Wilson at once identifies the inseparability of class and race prejudice in the North of the 1850s—in part through manipulating the literary convention of the "tragic mulatta"—and inscribes in her narrative a countermodel of interracial inclusion and national incorporation. This countermodel both takes part in and critiques the nationalist ideology of the concurrent common school movement of its day. The complex identifications Wilson negotiates positions Frado, finally, as the quintessential antebellum American—at an uncertain crossroads with respect to issues of race, nation, and class.

Ever since Henry Louis Gates Jr.'s groundbreaking rediscovery of Harriet Wilson's *Our Nig* in 1983, critics—beginning with Gates himself—have been riveted by the enigmatic nature of lines such as these from the novel's preface:[3] "I do not pretend to divulge every transaction in my own life, which the unprejudiced would declare unfavorable in comparison with treatment of legal bondmen; I have purposely omitted what would most provoke shame in our good anti-slavery friends at home."[4] Gates attributes "the text's lacunae, its silences and reticences" to the most perspicuous motivation—Wilson's desire to remain silent about the precise extent of the "white Northern racism" she experienced, which, "if depicted, could well result in an adverse reaction against Northern whites and could thereby do harm to the antislavery movement."[5]

To be sure, sexual exploitation and Northern race prejudice must account for much of Wilson's narrative hesitancy; however, a related but separate concern is also integral to our understanding of Wilson's authorial strategy of insisting on not "divulging" key "transactions" of her history. Indeed, the term "transactions," in its connection to emergent capitalist social relations, seems especially appropriate in the context of the little we are told directly about Wilson's forced familiarity with the public poor relief system of the nineteenth century. For example, from the testimonial by "Allida" in the text's appendix, we learn that before the birth of her son, "Alfrado" was reduced to seeking aid from "the institution, prepared for the *homeless*," as the protagonist herself describes the local poor farm in a letter that comprises part of Allida's testimony. Allida elaborates: "The charity on which she depended failed at last, and there was nothing to save her from the 'County House;' *go she must.*"[6] We also learn from Allida that Alfrado stayed in that institution until "the birth of her babe," George Mason Wilson. Beyond such direct references in the text's external apparatus, however, there are few explicit allusions to antebellum poor relief, though Wilson's autobiographical novel itself constitutes a veritable historical dramatization of the limitations of the system that could also "provoke shame in our good anti-slavery friends at home."

As if to underscore her intentions in the preface to suppress material she considers capable of producing "shame" in her readers, Wilson refrains during the course of her story from employing the precise terms associated with public poor relief at midcentury. There do, however, appear indirect allusions to such public "assistance" methods, all of which occur toward the close of Wilson's narrative, when, as Gates notes, "the fiction, or the guise of her fictional account of her life, tends to fall away."[7] In one such instance, the narrator describes with obvious derision the "removal" of the ailing Frado to the home of a Mrs. Hoggs: "Mrs. Hoggs was a lover of gold and silver, and she asked the favor of filling her coffers by caring for the sick. The removal caused severe sickness." Earlier, after Frado's famous confrontation with Mrs. Bellmont, in which she threatens "never to work a mite more" for her tyrannical mistress, she contemplates running away but decides instead to stay "through her period of service, which would expire when she was eighteen years of age."[8]

All of the aforementioned social arrangements, including the indentured servitude alluded to in the latter case, constitute various forms of "outdoor" and "indoor" poor relief. "Indoor relief," or the establishment of county poorhouses, eventually superseded the practice known as the "New England method" or "outdoor relief," wherein the destitute were auctioned off to private homes by the bidder who offered to maintain the "pauper" or "orphan" at the lowest public expense.[9] However, a significant period of overlap ensued, in which both institutions continued congruently. Moreover, according to a study of the poor relief system in the counties around Milford, New Hampshire, where Wilson is believed to have grown up, the practice known variously as "venduing," "letting out," or "binding out" was not confined to adults: "Often, the child was auctioned off like the adult paupers to the lowest bidder. At other times the child was 'bound out' to local farmers, artisans, sea captains, or housewives for a certain period of time. Written indentures in the form of contracts were signed to ensure fair play and to benefit the child."[10]

Further external evidence that Wilson was likely to have been "bound out" can be found in a local history of Goffstown, New Hampshire, the location of the poor farm where the author gave birth to her child. George Plummer Hadley's *The*

History of the Town of Goffstown, 1733–1920 records that "over-seers of the poor had authority to bind out idle or poor persons or set them to work—males to twenty-one and females to eighteen years of age"—the age at which Frado completes her service.[11] Given this documentation, there remains little doubt that Wilson's acquaintance with the deprivations and humiliations of the antebellum poor relief system—both the "outdoor" and "indoor" methods—was intimate and long-standing.[12]

Thus far, however, commentators have chosen to fore-ground either the theme of Northern racism sustained in *Our Nig*, its conflicted relation to the slave narrative tradition, its subversion of sentimental conventions, or some combination of these. In the process, these studies have yet fully to explore the relation between such social and textual formations and the au-thor's experience of economic hardship and class alienation and how the complex subjectivity Frado embodies might find repre-sentational expression in the narrative.[13] Before turning to the novel itself, therefore, it would seem fruitful to delve further into the precise workings of the institution of poor relief at midcentury so as to underscore the resonances between the condition of slavery and economic privation for Northern "free" blacks and destitute whites. To do this, it is necessary to quote at length from the 1901 publication of *The History of Mil-ford*, written by New Hampshire historian George Ramsdell. His account describes the town's "outdoor relief" system in some detail: "The town's poor were sold at auction, as it was called, as in other towns, i.e. once a year, usually at the close of the annual town meeting, the moderator officiating as auction-eer, the public was called upon to say at what price per week or year the support of each pauper would be assumed. The first offer constituted the first bid, and thereafter the auctioneer called for lower and still lower bids, until it was evident that no lower figure could be reached, when the maintenance of the pauper was struck off to the lowest bidder." In a noteworthy ad-

dendum to this description, Ramsdell elaborates on the carnival/
slave auction atmospherics of such annual gatherings. He
records that the moderator of the town meetings was usually the
parish minister, who would also act as auctioneer. Ramsdell
continues: "To help along the bidding, the auctioneer held in his
hand a decanter filled (at the commencement of the sale) with
new rum, repeatedly calling attention to the bead upon the
liquor and to the rule of the sale that every bidder was entitled
to a glass of spirit. The writer had this from an eye witness."[14]

It is unlikely that any greater degree of dignity than what is
represented here was afforded those who, like Wilson, found
themselves housed at the Goffstown poorhouse, established in
1823. Hadley's two-volume history of Goffstown, published in
1922, recalls that the "code of by-laws" the town ratified for the
maintenance of the institution made explicit provisions for various forms of "punishment," including a practice that allowed
subjects to be "fettered and shackled and put into a dark hole or
place provided for that purpose and fed on bread and water for
a term not exceeding six days." By 1830, a new code of bylaws
had been instituted to accord with a revision in state law. The
reformed guidelines specified that "no punishment should ex-
ceed hard labor" and that "solitary confinement should not ex-
ceed forty-eight hours." Such officially authorized brutality
suggests a further dimension to Wilson's subtitle, *Showing That
Slavery's Shadows Fall Even Here.* The racism and abuse of power
Wilson exposes in her tale of Frado's servitude cannot meaningfully be severed from her coextensive experience with the punitive consequences of extreme poverty and class prejudice.[15]

It is important to note, as we turn to Wilson's novel, that the
practice of indenturing a free black girl to a white family was
not uncommon, especially considering the extra economic bur-
dens faced by free blacks in Northern cities in the 1850s. James
Oliver affirms that even for socially advantaged mulattoes in
such cities as Buffalo and Boston, "the local social and economic

conditions made it almost impossible for them to find skilled jobs."[16] Considering such circumstances, it is not surprising that the town records of nearby Madbury, New Hampshire, contain an account of "a Negro Girl Named Nancy Being free Born in Said Parish and She Destitute of Father or Mother or any other Relations to Help her" being "apprenticed" to a "Patience Hill" for nine years.[17]

MAG'S CLASS DOWNFALL AND THE "TRAGIC MULATTA" NARRATIVE

In some respects, there are notable plot similarities between *Our Nig* and the conventional "tragic mulatto" tale. While situated in the "free" North rather than in the slave South, the novel recounts the trials and eventual downfall of its protagonist, Frado, who, like her literary predecessors, is abandoned by her parents, one of whom is black. Left to the nefarious devices of the brutal Bellmont family, she seeks comfort from two well-meaning but ineffectual abolitionist sons and finds solace in the local public school until she is old enough to fend for herself. After trying her hand unsuccessfully at various means of employment, Frado is eventually vanquished by years of physical abuse and extreme poverty. The story begins and ends with the author's urgent plea to the reader to support her literary endeavor.

More often, however, commentators have tended to remark upon the dissimilarities between Wilson's work and the typical chronicle of the doomed mulatta. Among such discontinuities is the fact that Frado's mother, Mag, is white. The usual plot calls for the maternal figure to be herself a light-skinned product of plantation concubinage who has either died or is soon absent from the novelistic action. By contrast, *Our Nig* instead begins with the story of the seduction and abandonment of Mag, a white woman. Indeed, but for her racial status, the scenes of betrayal that befall Frado's mother at the commencement of Wilson's narrative follow the traditional "tragic mulatta" story line. Here, though, the primary issue is not race but the class downfall that accompanies illicit sexuality. Consequently, the narration is replete with the terms of material gain and loss, rise and fall. Herself orphaned at a tender age, Mag longs for the affection of an unnamed suitor, a longing that "whispered of an elevation before unaspired to." The voice of "her charmer, so ravishing, sounded far above her. It seemed like an angel's, alluring her upward and onward. She thought she could ascend to him and become an equal. She surrendered to him a priceless gem, which he proudly garnered as a trophy, with those of other victims, and left her to her fate."[18] The repeated allusions in these lines to the exchange value of sexual virtue prefigures a focus on class relations that becomes inseparable from the discourse of race, especially after the introduction of Jim, Mag's black admirer. Three sentences later, following the condensed style of the narrative, Mag gives birth to an infant, who soon dies. Her response, that "God be thanked" since "no one can taunt *her* with my ruin," rehearses a common trope in the "tragic mulatta" tradition, in which characters either express or carry out a wish to "save" their newborns—through death—from the cruel fate that awaits them. Recall Archy's near-murder of his offspring in *The Slave* and Cassy's story of poisoning her infant in *Uncle Tom's Cabin.* By transposing onto a white woman's body elements of the "tragic mulatto" convention, Wilson at once challenges her readers and the convention itself. In other words, not only does the author invert the normative paradigm of the sexualized, objectified mulatta, she also establishes a necessary correlation between class and race prejudice that will intensify as the narrative progresses.

Of course, this early section of *Our Nig* also recalls the seduction novels of the eighteenth century whose primary function, as Cathy N. Davidson has shown, is to portray the ruination of their female protagonists and thereby serve as both cautionary tale and moral compass for their female readership concerning the dangers of sexual transgression.[19] However, by the third page of Wilson's work, a crucial distinction becomes manifest between the cultural work *Our Nig* sets out to perform and that carried out by its eighteenth-century precursors. In telling language, the narrator relates that "Mag's new home was contaminated by the publicity of her fall; she had a feeling of degradation oppressing her." Here, the moral culpability rests not with the novel's protagonist but with those who have "contaminated" and spread "publicity of her fall"—by the social formation that causes her to feel a "degradation oppressing her." This sense of wider social responsibility for Mag's reduced circumstances is magnified in the direct address to the reader that follows: "Alas, how fearful are we to be first in extending a helping hand to those who stagger in the mires of infamy; to speak the first words of hope and warning to those emerging into the sunlight of morality! Who can tell what numbers, advancing just far enough to hear a cold welcome and join in the reserved converse of *professed reformers*, disappointed, disheartened, have chosen to dwell in unclean places, rather than encounter these 'holier-than-thou' of the great brotherhood of man!"[20]

In these lines, Wilson indicts the self-righteous, "holier than thou" posture of the "great brotherhood of man," who offer the needy no more than "a cold welcome." More than that, she laments the unfulfilled promise of such "professed reformers," whose rhetoric, rather than offering succor, merely "disappoint[s] and "dishearten[s]." The narrator thus delineates an unpleasant choice for "those who stagger in the mires of infamy" between joining in the "reserved converse" of the purported altruists and continuing instead "to dwell in unclean places." In doing so, she directly associates the activities of such "reformers" with the idea of a "dwelling place," or home, as the central locus of their intended missions of charity. Timothy Dodge explains that the evangelical reform movements that

flourished from 1820 until the Civil War produced a new attitude of "moral fundamentalism" that encompassed the administration of poor relief: "Since poverty was now perceived as a
major new problem, the older methods of its relief were called
into question. *Reformers* saw poverty as caused by the weakness
of an individual's character or body. It was a curable condition.
The solution was to build up a pauper's character rather than to
just relieve his need. Reformers had come up with a solution:
the almshouse."[21]

It is this pious, punitive demeanor that appears to be the
most immediate object of Wilson's invective in the preceding
passage from the novel, an attitude she knew from experience
helped to foster the deplorable conditions at the local poorhouse and that prompted Mag to vow to "ask no favors of familiar faces; to die neglected and forgotten before she would be
dependent on any."[22] Dodge continues: "The almshouse became
popular at the same time as the penitentiary and the insane asy-
lum. Institutional confinement was the answer for some of society's ills. Reformers thought that the almshouse experience
could actually rehabilitate the poor."[23] Wilson's authorial vehemence was no doubt bolstered by the fact that this period
marked the burgeoning of county poorhouses. In some cases, as
with the nearby Goffstown home, the various types of institutions were merged together. George Plummer Hadley recounts
that "by the by-laws it will be seen that the poorhouse was made
a place of detention and punishment for criminals and disor-
derly persons, and they should be subject to the rules and regu-
lations thereof." Elsewhere, he comments: "The town farm was
an improvement on the former methods of caring for the poor,
yet it was no delectable resort for the aged and infirm, nor an
elysian field for those who could labor. The worthy poor, pauper, insane, and criminals were all together; no separate apart-
ment for mildly insane or the unfortunate. The same tasks and
the same tables were their lot."[24]

Such an assessment helps us appreciate more clearly the reason for Mag's preoccupation in the early sections of *Our Nig* with losing her means of subsistence, and thus her home, albeit "a hovel she had often passed in better days."[25] Though we know little of what Harriet Wilson actually knew of her mother's past, we do know that the writer herself had ample experience with the consequences of homelessness at midcentury. In a letter responding to the novel, Lydia Maria Child articulates her awareness of the barbarity associated with almshouses and places the requirement of appropriate housing paramount: "How to find a home for such outcasts as poor Mag is a very difficult problem. Public institutions are generally anything but healing to their wounded souls, and it is rare to find a family all the members of which are disposed to help them forget the past. . . . [I]s it not strange that some way cannot be discovered by which the elements of human society can be so harmonized as to prevent such frightful discords?"[26] Engaged throughout her life in a range of social activism beyond abolition, Child here demonstrates her understanding of Wilson's aim in *Our Nig* to draw vital connections between the economic privation and race prejudice both Mag and Frado are unremittingly forced to endure.

Those connections are brought into stark relief with the ensuing marriage of Mag and Jim. If it was not unusual for white families in the North to indenture orphaned and indigent black children like Frado, the portrayal of miscegenation in *Our Nig* that produces Frado in the first place is extremely rare in literary history. The matter-of-fact tone with which Wilson depicts the union of Frado's white mother, Mag, and Jim, a free black laborer and a "kind-hearted African," is unprecedented in either the slave narrative or the sentimental traditions. Gates proclaims that "never . . . was miscegenation depicted with any degree of normality before *Our Nig*" and attributes the obscurity to which the novel fell victim in part to "its unabashed representation of interracial marriage."[27] For her part, Frances Smith Foster has argued that "the description of this union subverts the tradition of interracial relationships common to literature by whites. Far from being sympathetic, this depiction bears the fine flavor of cynicism."[28] Such commentaries have failed to consider the import of the humor that pervades the scenes of Jim contemplating his proposal to Mag. The playful authorial tone evinced in Jim's spontaneous utterances of determination overheard by the shop owner ("by golly!") is rare in the novel generally and especially in the chapters concerning Mag's history. As such, it would seem to indicate an attitude more like ambivalence than cynicism on the part of Wilson toward the interraciality depicted in the novel. Indeed, this section of the text sets out for itself the ambitious project of dramatizing the confusion of discourses that results when the hegemonic ideologies of class and race stratification to which Jim and Mag are both subject clash with sentimental romantic conventions.

For example, Jim's assessment that Mag would "be as much of a prize to me as she'd fall short of coming up to the mark with white folks" conflates the language of exchange value and class status with the sentimental discourse of romantic love that characterizes Jim's speech throughout his brief appearance in the narrative. Similarly, when Jim makes his marriage declaration, asserting that "I's black outside, I know, but I's got a white heart inside," and asks Mag, "Which you rather have, a black heart in a white skin, or a white heart in a black one?" the romantic context challenges the essentialism of racial categories as much as it rehearses such binaries. Because of her history, however, Mag is demonstrably less hopeful than Jim about the possibility of transgressing prevailing social structures and their constitutive discourses. Her reply to Jim's proposal—"I can do but two things . . . beg my living or get it from you"—conveys the degree to which her vision has been restricted to seeing her options as strictly material choices, both of which seem to her to constitute a downfall. It is notable in the context of our interest in the relation of *Our Nig* to antebellum poor relief that Jim prevails only after promising Mag that "I can give you a better home than this, and not let you suffer so."[29] The direct address that closes the chapter does indeed "bear the fine flavor of cynicism," but not in the sense Foster intends. The narrator reproves her audience: "You can philosophize, gentle reader, upon the impropriety of such unions, and preach dozens of sermons on the evils of amalgamation. Want is a more powerful philosopher and preacher. Poor Mag. She has sundered another bond which held her to her fellows. She had descended another step down the ladder of infamy."[30] Here, "want" is positioned as a "more powerful philosopher and preacher" than sermons against "amalgamation." It functions as moral persuasion over against a vision that sees interracial union as only base, material, and instrumental. That is to say that "want" teaches Mag to disdain pious pronouncements about "amalgamation." The change in tone from the blunt, declarative language of the first half of the address to the ornate, melodramatic diction of the concluding lines suggests a corresponding shift toward an ironic authorial distance. The tone of sentimental excess in the sentences following "Poor Mag," delivered in flamboyant metaphors of social descent and exile, suggest Wilson's perspicacity about interlocking systems of class and race prejudice and her impatience with the casual malignity of the majority culture's subjugation.

Again in the following chapter, Wilson vacillates between the lexical economy of the marketplace and that of romantic love. Jim is described as being "proud of his treasure,—a white wife," at the same time as the reader is informed that "he loved Mag to the last." Jim's death provokes her, already despairing, into a state of spiritual bankruptcy. Once more invoking the tone of sentimental excess that signifies social censure, the narrator recounts Mag's descent into "the darkness of perpetual infamy" that accompanies her ensuing marriage to Jim's black business partner, Seth. When the couple discusses the need to "give their children away," we are introduced for the first time to Frado, "a beautiful mulatto, with long, curly, and handsome, roguish eyes, sparkling with an exuberance of spirit almost beyond restraint."[31] This physical description of the novel's main protagonist, with its emphasis on the exotic beauty of the child's facial features and its reference to a quality of effusive energy and animation, recalls the prototype of the literary mulatta we have seen repeatedly in this study.

SUBJECTIVITY AND SOCIAL INCLUSIVENESS

At the same time, however, Frado departs importantly from the convention of the fated, passive "tragic mulatta" figure. Though undoubtedly of mixed race, in many ways she defies the designation "tragic," despite her life circumstances of economic and emotional depravation. Soon after arriving at the Bellmonts, for example, Frado deliberates about whether to stay to face the abuse she knows awaits her. The narrator observes that the young girl "was of a wilful, determined nature, a stranger to fear, and would not hesitate to wander away should she decide to."[32] Moreover, as we shall see, Frado's agency gains force through the course of the novel, a trajectory that constitutes the reverse of the conventional "tragic mulatta" narrative. Though many commentators place the emergence of Frado's full subjectivity at the moment late in *Our Nig* when she finally challenges Mrs. Bellmont's authority, I see it as flourishing within the benevolent, nurturing environment of the public school she attends over Mrs. Bellmont's objections.[33] This portion of the novel has been underexamined, yet it is pivotal in Wilson's artistic and political vision. Located at the center of the narrative, the public school depicted in *Our Nig* extends the principle of moral education that was so important to antebellum common school reform to encompass racial as well as class egalitarianism.

Ultimately, Wilson offers an implicit critique and rebuke in her portrait of public school progressivism of the race- and class-bound nature of the reformist movement. As beneficiaries of the poor relief system of indenture, the Bellmonts were legally obligated to provide a minimum amount of schooling for their female servant. According to historian Marcus Wilson Jernegan, an eighteenth-century New Hampshire law stipulated that town selectmen, or "overseers of the poor," were ordered to include a clause in indenture contracts to the effect that "'for the Benefit of Such Children; at the least that the Master be Instructed to teach Males to read and write, and the Females to read.'" The statute also makes clear that "a penalty of removal might fall on parents and masters who neglected the education of their children or apprentices."[34] In later decades, after the advent of public education, "masters of apprentices, if they chose, might conform to the requirement for education as set forth in the indenture by sending an apprentice to a free school."[35] The narrator of *Our Nig* portrays the decision to allow Frado to attend school as a rare triumph of Mr. Bellmont's paternal authority, noting, "'The word once spoken admitted of no appeal. . . . [T]he word became law."[36] The usually timid patriarch's rare forcefulness suggests that his command stands in for such juridical mandates, whether or not they were usually followed in the case of black indentured servants. The fact that Miss Marsh, the schoolteacher, is portrayed as a committed reformer both gestures toward the contemporaneous common school movement and critiques it for not expanding its liberal philosophy explicitly to include a more expansive notion of social difference.

Continuing the motif of social ascent and descent, Mary, Mrs. Bellmont's spiteful daughter, sees in Frado's arrival at school "a fair prospect of lowering Nig where, according to her views, she belonged."[37] Indeed, considering the mistreatment Frado has thus far endured at the hands of the Bellmont family, the reader expects her to be the victim of more of the same in the social confines of the school yard, where her position of race and class disenfranchisement makes her an easy target for Mary and her peers. Initially, our fears appear to be warranted: "As soon as she appeared, with scanty clothing and bared feet, the children assembled, noisily published her approach: 'See that nigger,' shouted one. 'Look! look!' cried another. 'I won't play with her,' said one little girl. 'Nor I neither,' replied another.'" However, just when Frado has all but decided to turn around and return "home," Miss Marsh, the teacher, surprises both the novel's readership and the protagonist herself with a signal act of welcome: "[O]bserving the downcast looks of the child, [she] took her by the hand, and led her into the school-room." Once inside, Miss Marsh delivers a lecture to her students that constitutes the only explicit condemnation in the novel of "all prejudice" and thus merits quoting in full: "She then reminded them of their duties to the poor and friendless; their cowardice in attacking a young innocent child; referred them to one who looks not on outward appearances, but on the heart. 'She looks like a good girl; I think *I* shall love her, so lay aside all prejudice, and vie with each other in shewing kindness and good-will to one who seems different from you,' were the closing remarks of the kind lady. Those kind words! The most agreeable sound which ever meets the ear of sorrowing, grieving childhood."[38]

This speech is remarkable in several ways and marks a crucial turning point in *Our Nig*. First, it is singular in that it calls attention not to racial difference solely, as one would expect, but rather to the students' "duties to the poor and friendless" generally. It urges them to renounce "all prejudice" and to show compassion "to one who seems different." In its inclusiveness, then, the address encompasses the differences of race *and* class that Frado embodies and resists eliding one in favor of the other. It suggests that to Wilson, the experience of indenture and the experience of race prejudice are inextricable from and integral to one another and must be treated as such.

In addition, the figure of Miss Marsh herself serves an extraordinary function in the narrative, and one that is often overlooked. Though she appears only briefly, she is the sole character in the novel proper during the period of Frado's indenture to operate outside the sphere of the Bellmont family. In fact, as a public school teacher, she alone represents a morally rejuvenated public sphere in accordance with the ascendant Protestant, nationalist ideology that marked the new system of public schooling in New England. Christian (that is, Protestant) morality, self-discipline, and cultural uniformity constituted the hallmarks of the common school reform movement even as it perpetuated virulent discrimination against blacks and new European immigrants. Wilson's portrait of Miss Marsh as radical social reformer represents her critique of the limitations associated with public school reform and her clear sense that it was the public sector's obligation to intervene to achieve social justice.

Thus, within the bounds of the school yard, Wilson depicts a model social system in which "shewing kindness and goodwill" by promoting racial and class equity is demanded of all "citizens." Most striking is the manner in which the teacher's leadership has immediate and profound effects in promoting an alternative egalitarian social order in the realm of the public schoolhouse: "Example rendered her words efficacious. Day by day there was a manifest change of deportment towards 'Nig.' Her speeches often drew merriment from the children; no one could do more to enliven their favorite pastimes than Frado."[39]

Under the empowering influence of Miss Marsh, therefore, Frado thrives, transforming herself not just from silent object to speaking subject but also to a position of community leadership. As Frado's stature increases, Mary's social capital correspondingly declines: "Mary could not endure to see [Frado] thus noticed, yet knew not how to prevent it. She could not influence her schoolmates as she wished. She had not gained their affections by winning ways and yielding points of controversy."[40] In this way, school is figured as the place where Frado is given the fullest license to employ her manifest skills at social interaction and rhetorical proficiency. The character once approximating "tragic mulatta" status has now been transformed to an exalted position among her peers through the intervention of a reformative state in the person of Miss Marsh.

Mary, not satisfied with the "abuse and taunts" to which she subjects Frado on the way home, resolves to use physical force " 'to subdue her,' to 'keep her down.' "[41] Wilson's use of quotation marks around these two phrases underscores their purpose as the stock vocabulary of race and class subjugation. In the episode that follows, Mary attempts to tyrannize Frado by forcing her to cross the stream on "a single plank." The scheme backfires, however, when Mary herself loses her footing and falls in. More significant than Mary's blunder itself is her classmates' response to the event. The narrator records that "some of the larger scholars being in sight, ran, and thus prevented Mary from drowning and Frado from falling."[42] In this scene, Mary's attempt to exert class and race dominion over Frado fails twice— once in the actual execution and again because the children, now transformed by Miss Marsh's influence, rescue both playmates at once rather than making distinctions based on social ranking or race. The students demonstrate the import of enacting a progressive public social structure founded on principles of equality that go beyond the republican individualism of typical antebellum school reform. In a larger sense, the novel argues for reinvigorated public-sector interventions to bring about such social reforms.

Accordingly, public school constitutes the site of Frado's greatest opportunity for self-expression and fulfillment. The narrator underscores the contrast between the protagonist's deportment in Mrs. Bellmont's presence, when she is "under restraint," to her behavior in class, where "the pent up fires burst forth": "She was ever at some sly prank when unseen by her teacher, in school hours; not unfrequently [*sic*] some outburst of merriment, of which she was the original, was charged upon some innocent mate, and punishment was inflicted which she merited. They enjoyed her antics so fully that any of them would suffer wrongfully to keep open the avenues of mirth. She would venture far beyond propriety, thus shielded and countenanced."[43] Here, Frado adopts the social persona of the mischievous rebel precisely because she is "shielded and countenanced" by a collectivity where acceptance and equality are required. Later, Wilson returns to the subject of the emancipatory potential of the public school when Mrs. Bellmont scolds her husband for allowing Frado to learn to read: "I found her reading the Bible to-day, just as though she expected to turn pious nigger, and preach to white folks. So now you see what good comes of sending her to school."[44] Lawrence A. Cremin, among many others, has argued that while "social harmony was a chief goal of popular education" at the time, so was "industrial discipline." Students learned "the grouping, periodizing, and objective impersonality [that] were not unlike the factory."[45] However, to Mrs. Bellmont, Frado's experience at public school poses an immediate threat to existing hierarchies of race and class. Following the convention of antislavery literature, education—and especially literacy—is always represented as the greatest challenge to prevailing structures of power in the novel. Wilson's innovation is to focus on the emerging institution of the public school as the place where Frado is allowed her fullest agency. In these scenes, then, the author offers an alternative to the Protestant conformity of common school reform ideology. In its place is rendered a truly liberatory vision of social institutions in general and an emancipatory role for the public school in particular.

If Frado's dynamic subjectivity in these scenes seems to counter the passivity of the conventional "tragic mulatta" figure, it also contests that aspect of the tradition that requires that such female characters accord with the nineteenth-century ideal of "true womanhood."[46] Here, as elsewhere in the novel, Frado's actions fall far short of such expectations of femininity. Indeed, the very androgyny of her name accentuates that fact, as does the parallel between "Frado" and "Fido," the protagonist's loyal dog. As Cynthia Davis notes, for Wilson's heroine, "the primary and delineating experience is not sexuality, but pain."[47] At the same time, as the foregoing episodes suggest and as we see throughout *Our Nig*, Frado is adept at incorporating into her experience of victimization occasions for resistance and tricksterism.

In one such incident, Mrs. Bellmont seeks to put Frado in her place when she sees her seated "in her mistress' chair" eating her dinner after the rest of the family has finished. She commands Frado to eat from her used plate instead of the clean one for which Frado had been reaching when Mrs. Bellmont entered the room. Frado, indignant about "being commanded to do what was disagreeable by her mistress *because* it was disagreeable," calls in Fido, who licks the plate "to the best of his ability." Only then does she "proceed[ ] to eat her dinner."[48] However, a problem develops as Frado's tricksterism relates to the Bellmont brothers, James and Jack, as is demonstrated in the denouement of the above-mentioned episode: "James came to hear the kitchen version of the affair. Jack was boiling over with laughter. He related all the circumstances to James, and pulling a bright, silver half-dollar from his pocket, he threw it at Nig, saying, 'There, take that; 't was worth paying for.' "[49] Unlike the parity that eventuates among Frado and her classmates, the unbalanced power relations that obtain between Frado and the Bellmont brothers produce a pronounced atmospheric shift in which Frado's tricksterism verges into minstrelsy.

Indeed, James and Jack serve a complex purpose in Wilson's narrative. If Miss Marsh stands in for a reformed public sector, a reimagined social collectivity, then the Bellmont brothers represent status quo New England reformers—often either ineffectual or downright pernicious in matters of race and class reform.

To be sure, they come to Frado's defense in her ongoing struggle for survival against the staggering brutalities of Mrs. Bellmont. James, in particular, is instrumental in evoking in Frado a desire for Christian solace and salvation. Yet the vexed nature of Frado's relation to orthodox religion mirrors and often intersects with her ambiguous attachment to James himself. When she attends services with Aunt Abby, Mr. Bellmont's unmarried sister, for instance, Frado's reflections on her own moral and racial suitability for heaven are inextricably interpenetrated with her longing for physical proximity to the dying James. For example, not comprehending the minister's reference to repentance, Frado deliberates: "She knew she was unfit for any heaven, made for whites or blacks. She would gladly repent, or do anything which would admit her to share the abode of James."[50] The intensity of Frado's emotional allegiance to James, expressed here in terms of an unrequited desire to share his home, threatens to rehearse the standard "tragic mulatta" narrative with its overdetermined elements of sexualization and exploitative power dynamics.

In addition to offering Frado the consolation of religious instruction, James delivers impassioned speeches denouncing the racial oppression Frado seems fated to endure: "But to think how prejudiced the world are [sic] towards her people; that she must be reared in such ignorance as to drown all the finer feelings. When I think of what she might be, of what she will be, I feel like grasping time till opinions change, and thousands like her rise into a noble freedom. I have seen Frado's grief, because she is black, amount to agony."[51] Here, Wilson directly equates prejudice with the denial of education, a deprivation James mistakenly believes Frado has suffered. Yet the very context of this oration reveals the impotent nature of the brothers' patronage of Frado, since it is only delivered in direct response to Aunt Abby's urging that James take Frado home with him to Baltimore when he recovers from his illness. Though James responds that he intends to rescue Frado, he dies before the plan can be enacted.

On his deathbed, he counsels her: "[I]f you will be a good girl, and love and serve God, it will be but a short time before we are in a heavenly home together."[52] Once again, the allusion to a promised home together—however ethereal—suggests the concubinage of the "tragic mulatta" tradition. In this episode, Wilson deploys James's lecture to betray the morally uncertain nature of his version of evangelical Protestantism and to demonstrate the failure of Frado's supposed white protector to find for her a material remedy that will serve as a true home. More broadly, the scene illustrates the inadequacy of the prevailing systems of poor relief, since even with the most well meaning of white benefactors, the results are no better than under the paternalism of Southern plantation slavery.

Frado's indenture is referred to explicitly only when it is nearly over. Then, the narrator announces that "the approaching spring would close the term of years which Mrs. B claimed as the period of her servitude." Now ill from overwork and mistreatment, Frado doesn't fare well in domestic employment and is soon sent back to recover in the Bellmont's former workshop, where "cold and rain found unobstructed access." During her stay, Mrs. Bellmont makes clear that the family won't pay for the doctor's care: "You may look to the town for that, sir," she grumbles, in a reference to the prevailing system of local poor relief.[53]

Later in the novel, Frado's luck briefly appears to shift when "a friend" provides her with "a valuable recipe, from which she might herself manufacture a useful article for her maintenance." When the narrative ends, Frado is "busily employed in preparing her merchandise." It concludes with the an appeal for patronage that brings us back to where we began this discussion, with a concern for the consequences of textual omissions: "Still an invalid, she asks your sympathy, gentle reader. Refuse not, because some part of her history is unknown, save by Omniscient God. Enough has been unrolled to demand your sympathy and aid."

We learn from Allida's testimony in the appendix that the "valuable recipe" Frado acquires involves "restoring gray hair to its former color."[54] Much like autobiographical fiction itself, the "useful article"—a black dye—entails a kind of mediated recasting of the past. In this way, unlike the other profit-making ventures in which she engages, writing offers Frado/Wilson a means by which she can preserve her integrity (by telling her story but disclosing only what she chooses) and gain a measure of economic security—but only with the help of her "colored brethren universally" as well as a large number of "sympath[etic], gentle [white] reader[s]."[55]

Indeed, this allegorical element permeates Wilson's text. For example, after both Jane and Jack, the remaining Bellmont children, flee their repressive home, Frado laments that "there seemed no one capable of enduring the oppressions of the house but her."[56] The Bellmont residence is, after all, the "Two-Story White House, North" described in the novel's subtitle. Imaged thus, the structure functions as the national imaginary, with Frado, a poor black servant girl, its most burdened occupant. It is an architectural metaphor not merely or even primarily for the White House but more generally for the regional, racialized systems of labor that are invoked and implicitly paralleled throughout the work—Southern slavery on the one hand and Northern indenture on the other. The "two stories" are different by region but alike in that they are under the same "white" roof, the same racialized social order. Recalling the epic genre that relied so heavily on allegory, the protagonist journeys through twelve chapters of hardship and mortal testing to arrive at the moment of composition.

However, the point of this "epic"—unlike its canonical predecessors—is precisely *not* individual distinction and renown. Its chief goal, of course, is sheer material sustenance. Beyond that, however, it is to instill in its readers—black and white—a renewed vision of national purpose and civic responsibility, the same principles modeled by the public school teacher, Miss Marsh. Indeed, antebellum school reform was deeply invested in a vision of the Republic as both morally and nationally paramount. According to Cremin, the notion of America's superior destiny was intertwined with the educational values of equality and moral perfectibility, despite the realities of racial and gender repression. Indeed, nationalist sentiment went hand in hand with Protestant theology as twin hallmarks of common school education in the period. Students were taught that "their nation was destined to reach the peak of human civilization and, with God's help, to overcome all obstacles to material preeminence and spiritual elevation."[57] Judging from her narrative, Wilson believed in the redemptive potential of the public school movement— including its nationalizing function—even as she exposed its shortcomings with respect to the genuine extension of racial and class inclusion.

Moreover, judging by the testimonials in the appendix, the novel's strategy of exemplifying and inspiring a liberatory spirit of public inclusivity and collective responsibility appears to have been successful. For example, Allida instructs "all the friends who purchase a volume" to "remember they are doing good to one of the most worthy, and I had almost said most unfortunate, of the human family." In the second of the three accompanying letters, Margaretta Thorn deploys exactly the same lexical economy: "And now I would say, I hope those who call themselves friends of our dark-skinned brethren, will lend a helping hand, and assist our sister, not in giving, but in buying a book; the expense is trifling, and the reward of doing good is great. Our duty is to our fellow-beings, and when we let an opportunity pass, we know not what we lose."[58] Thus, neither of these testimonial writers views the activity of purchasing Wilson's book as charity or "giving." Instead, they define it as an act of civic "duty," of "doing good." It is the enactment of this revised concept of collective social responsibility to "the human family" and "our fellow-beings" that Wilson wants to supplant the demeaning practice of public charity. In so doing, she offers an alternative to the ascendant ideology of the marketplace. Though formulated as a means of escaping the humiliations of public relief, Wilson's efforts at authorship, it must be acknowledged, fail to the extent that her book was utterly ignored. Still, the fact that her story is disregarded is a measure of her audience's shortcomings, not her own.

Finally, although the quotation marks that frame the novel's pseudonymous signature, "Our Nig," have been much vaunted for their ironic resonances, it would seem worthwhile to focus our attention instead on the possessive cast of the title itself.[59] If we accept the allegorical component of the narrative, it is possible to see the collective plural "Our" in *Our Nig*, juxtaposed as it is with the overdetermined nationalist signification represented by the full subtitle, *Sketches from the Life of a Free Black, in a Two-Story White House, North, Showing That Slavery's Shadows Fall Even There*, as connoting exactly the kind of expansive, national sense of social responsibility advanced during the course of the narrative.[60] In other words, far from belonging to the Bellmonts alone, Frado serves the role of the nation's outcast child. More than that, she is the offspring of a white mother and a black father, so that in prevailing upon her readers to accept the mulatta foundling into the "national home," Wilson is concurrently asking us to accept into our national "family" the fact of interraciality—a proposition the majority of both races at midcentury found difficult to accept.

In several ways, then, *Our Nig* serves as a countertext and a corrective to the works that precede it in this study. For instance, the protagonist is unquestionably drawn from the sentimentalist tradition of the "tragic mulatto," yet in Wilson's revision of the narrative the issue of class relations is accented for the first time. The effect of this reworking is such that the mulatta heroine, though still victimized in other contexts, becomes, concurrently, the central agent in presenting the reader with a redemptive vision of society in which the distribution of power and the definition of the national collectivity are profoundly transformed. In addition, for the other reform writers examined here, the notion of interraciality is either placed in the service of a hierarchical, assimilationist vision of U.S. ascendancy, as in the case of Child, or, in Stowe's masterwork, introduced only to be eclipsed in favor of a racially homogeneous nationalist vision. In *Clotel*, Brown demonstrates the extent to which interraciality is constitutive of the nation's founding, yet, as with Hildreth's *The Slave*, American nationalism as it is presently conceived is finally indicted as incompatible with a biracial future. By contrast, Wilson is concerned with situating her mixed-race protagonist in her proper place in the "Two-Story White House, North." That is to say that she conceives of miscegenation and U.S. nationalism as not only coextensive but congruous. In this way, Wilson's text mounts a successful challenge to discursive traditions that in themselves are more diverse than has been previously acknowledged. If it is, perhaps, the broad scope of that challenge that finally proved too threatening to the novel's contemporaneous audience, then we would do well to attend to Wilson's work that much more closely today.

Coda

The "Tragic Mulatta" Then and Now

In July 2003, a front-page story appeared in the *New York Times* headlined "A Family Get-Together of Historic Proportions: Monticello Greets Kin of Jefferson's Slave." The story recounted the first reunion of the descendants of Sally Hemings ever to take place on the historic grounds of the Jefferson plantation. The newsworthiness of the event rested on the fact that its location granted legitimacy to long-standing claims that the third president of the United States had indeed fathered children with Hemings—a claim that was scientifically validated in 1998 when DNA evidence was published linking Jefferson to one of Hemings's sons and indicating that he might have fathered as many as five other Hemings children. The story featured a photo of scores of descendants of all hues and descriptions clustered in a circle holding hands. Despite this semblance of reconciliation and harmony, this most quintessentially American of family arguments persists. Indeed, more than a private family dispute, at issue, finally—literally and figuratively—is how American history will color its origins. Fully aware of the stakes, the Monticello Association, which administers the Jefferson cemetery and represents descendants of Thomas Jefferson and his wife, Martha, has disputed the DNA findings. Another organization, the Thomas Jefferson Heritage Society—also made up of Jefferson descendants—authorized its own panel, which concluded in 2001 that Randolph, the president's younger brother, was more likely to have been the father of Hemings's children.

Even distinguished historians have been reluctant to acknowledge the likelihood of Jefferson's patrimony. The *Times* story goes on to quote Jefferson biographer Joseph J. Ellis as asserting that "prior to the DNA, I'd say the case against Jefferson didn't reach beyond reasonable doubt."[1] For Ellis and many others, it took the imprimatur of genetic science to bring validity to the proposition that an aristocratic Virginia planter living in the late eighteenth and early nineteenth centuries was likely to have had sexual relations with a female bond servant. For some of Jefferson's posterity, the notion that one of the nation's "Founding Fathers" has a literal connotation remains unthinkable, despite the fact that, as historians of race have suggested, it would be anomalous for someone of Jefferson's southern patrician caste *not* to have engaged in such sexual liaisons, whether of long duration or not.[2] Indeed, the very persistence and intensity of the debate signal more than a concern over the reputation of the former president himself. Rather, they suggest the lasting nature of the fictions of race and racial hierarchies in American life and culture. More than that, they signify the enduring imbrication of race and American selfhood dating back to the nation's founding.

In other words, the fervor apparent in the contemporary drama over Jefferson's progeny bespeaks the enduring contest over interraciality in both familial and national contexts, which, at its core, comprises the essence of the "tragic mulatto" story. If we view the figure—as the antislavery writers in this study clearly did—as a literal embodiment of the contradictions inherent in the early republic between founding principles of equality and freedom on the one hand and brute racial subjugation on the other, then the story of Thomas Jefferson's "dusky Sally"—as William Wells Brown knew—is not only the earliest instance of a "tragic mulatta" narrative, it is *the* "tragic mulatta" narrative par excellence. Its stature as such is confirmed by its cultural and discursive tenacity: two hundred years after the legendary scandal erupted in the press, popular films continue to appear offering various renderings of the pairing and what the couple represented to each other—and thus to the country's sense of itself.[3] Public interest in the matter gained momentum at the turn into the twenty-first century, especially with the impetus of the DNA revelations. These contemporary film versions of the Jefferson-Hemings story demonstrate the ongoing resonance of the "tragic mulatto" emblem in popular imaginings about race. More precisely, they constitute important sites of ideological struggle over the contending significations of the trope in the mainstream U.S. imagination over time.

Two of these popular film renditions, *Jefferson in Paris* (1995) and the CBS television miniseries *Sally Hemings: An American Scandal* (2000), tell the story of Jefferson's tenure in Paris as minister to France, during which stay he is thought to have first become sexually involved with Hemings. While these productions both concern themselves with roughly the same historical material, their divergent representations of the pivotal characters in this originary "tragic mulatta" tale merit further consideration and comparison. As products of Hollywood and network television, respectively, both versions are under pressure to foreground the "love-story" plot, which the historical record makes possible. Predictably, then, *Jefferson in Paris*, starring Nick Nolte as the title character and Thandie Newton as Sally, is advertised as "an impassioned story of forbidden love." The more recent *Sally Hemings: An American Scandal*, starring Sam Neill and Carmen Ejogo, was picketed by antiracist viewers angry at its ad campaign, which declared the film "the greatest love story never told." In her account of the making of the miniseries, screenwriter and co-executive producer Tina Andrews recalls protestors' indignation that the "tone of the piece [was] being presented as a 'love story.' "[4] In addition to responding to a commercial impetus, the romantic imperative in the Jefferson/Hemings drama and how it is enacted in these works function as a metaphor for exploring more essential issues of interraciality and nationhood, especially if we examine these themes in light of the "tragic mulatta" narrative frame. The ambiguity over whether the liaison can meaningfully be termed a "love story" can be seen as a figure for the unceasing and ineradicable American anxiety about the extent to which the Republic was founded on its much-vaunted ideals of liberty or, rather, on a history of racial repression and violence. In such productions, Sally Hemings as "tragic mulatta" acts as both embodiment of and as mediator between these ideological poles. Elements of a love story act to recuperate the possibility of a romantic vision of national origins as much as images of white supremacy and black resistance threaten such a notion.

Significantly, the preponderance of the action in both adaptations of the affair takes place abroad, in Europe, away from the legal constraints of American slave laws. Both Sally and her brother, James, who precedes her arrival in Paris, are regarded as free subjects as long as they remain on French soil. Thus, as with the conclusion of *Clotel*, the question of the personal liberty of the slave is necessarily conjoined with a departure from America's confines, with alienation from the homeland. Unlike *Clotel*, however, the film version of Hemings's association with Jefferson is decidedly a romance—and a romance with a willing sexual ingenue. In *Jefferson in Paris*, an infatuated Sally seduces her reserved master as much as the reverse. She regales a supine and sleepy Jefferson with a minstrelsy-inspired ghost story about a slave who drowned herself in a Monticello pond and who Sally fears has followed her across the Atlantic. Jefferson visibly softens when Sally recalls that upon seeing the phantom, "My hair 'ris up till I couldn't get my hat back on my head." She proceeds to approach her master's bed, pretending to fan away a fly until

Jefferson stills her wrist and looks meaningfully into her eyes. A discreet jump cut to a dinner-party scene follows. In a later episode, Jefferson stills Sally's hand again, this time when she bends to unbuckle his shoes before he retires. She quietly replaces her master's hand back on his knee before continuing to loosen his shoes. In scenes such as these, the dynamic between Jefferson and Hemings in this reinterpretation of her as "tragic mulatta" is one of paternalist affection toward an enslaved, yet innocent and enamored young woman.[5] At one point, Jefferson offers to pay Sally 24 francs a month for her domestic service and then suggests that she store the money in his own desk drawer for safe-keeping. There is no doubt, however, that Nick Nolte's representation of the Founding Father is meant to be a sympathetic, vulnerable one throughout. In a still later scene, he inquires gently of his slave: "You still scared of me, Sally?" She responds, demurely, "I ain't scared of you, massa." To be sure, the Jefferson depicted in *Jefferson in Paris* is first and foremost a lover, not a slaveholder.[6]

Elsewhere, the incestuous excess that figures so prominently in the "tragic mulatta" genre and that we saw delineated most starkly in Richard Hildreth's *The Slave* manifests itself bizarrely in this production. According to historical accounts, Jefferson was accompanied to Paris by his eldest daughter, Martha, named after the future president's recently deceased wife. Martha was Sally's half-sister, since they shared the same father.[7] In the film, when Jefferson receives word that another of his daughters has died of whooping cough at home in Monticello, he has Polly, Martha's younger sister, brought to France with Sally to console Martha and himself. A strange antipathy then develops between Martha and Sally, especially when it concerns Jefferson's affections. Martha, as played by Gwyneth Paltrow, bestows proprietary attentions on her father that betray a nearly libidinous jealousy. Upon the arrival of Polly and Sally to Paris, Martha kneels before her father, clutching him and vowing, "You shall always, always above everything be first in my life." Concerning Polly she exclaims, "I will be her nurse and her sister and her mother and her everything and your everything, dearest Pappa." Here, strangely, the unseemly incestuousness of plantation concubinage that is such a powerful theme in the "tragic mulatto" tradition is transferred from the relatively faultless and benevolent Jefferson to the covetous rivalry of his daughter, Martha. Within this internal filmic logic, Jefferson's love for Sally is presented as less taboo than the subterranean erotic tension between father and daughter. It is as if the pervasive moral corruption endemic to the slavocracy is able to surface only covertly and indirectly under the pressure of the film to present Jefferson and Hemings as "forbidden" but appealing paramours.

Thus, *Jefferson in Paris* presents the pair as amorous companions, with the hero as reluctant and conflicted overlord. The film dramatizes most explicitly Jefferson's ambivalent awareness of the racial power dynamics at play in a scene depicting a confrontation among both Hemings siblings (James and Sally) and Jefferson prior to the future president's return to America. James prevails on his sister to stay in Paris and enjoy her newfound freedom with him rather than go back to Virginia a slave.[8] Sally, now pregnant, is nonetheless depicted as confused and torn. Her master/lover prevails upon her to accompany him, addressing her as though he were a conventional suitor and promising her an impossibly elevated class station: "Don't you want to be mistress of Monticello?" he implores. "Monticello is yours, as I am," she replies, in a piece of dialogue that artfully conjoins political savvy with erotic devotion. In response, Jefferson appeals to her as her admirer and intimate exclusively: "You are my true light and my true love, and everything that is best in me belongs to you," he pledges, adopting the role of gentleman courtier in place of property holder. The very performance of romance between white master/lover and slave that is an essential element of the "tragic mulatta" narrative tradition is central to this mass media rendering of the Jefferson and Hemings liaison. Moreover, its persistence is evidence of the figure's potency as a measure of the nation's deep-seated contradictions between its idealized past and its racialized history. The aim of nineteenth-century versions of such asymmetric sexual dynamics was to underscore the iniquity of slavery. Yet to the extent that such mulatta fiction gets recuperated as modern-day stories of "forbidden love," it offers a fantasy of white redemption.

While its central plot is similar to *Jefferson in Paris*, the portrayal of the title character in *Sally Hemings: An American Scandal* allows for a complication—if not a revision—of the love-story imperative. Notably, producer Tina Andrews was herself embroiled in an interracial sex scandal of sorts in the 1980s. As one of the first black women soap opera actors, she was fired after the audience reacted badly following the first-ever daytime kiss between the races.[9] In Andrews's rendering of the Jefferson legend, Sally is considerably more self-possessed, arguing with Jefferson about racial politics and at one point even deriding him for his condemnation of "amalgamation" in *Notes on the State of Virginia*. This time, when Sally is asked to choose whether to safeguard her freedom in France or return to Monticello, her first reaction is one of defiance, though she ultimately relents: "I won't give birth to a slave," she tells Jefferson. "I'm free now and I want my child to be free." The scene abruptly changes at this juncture to the street riots that erupted at the start of the French Revolution, the event that precipitated Jefferson's return to Monticello. As the carriage bearing Jefferson and Sally away navigates through the tumultuous crowds, a leader of the revolt addresses himself first to the ambassador and then to Sally herself, whom he has encountered before. In a moment that gestures toward the film's awareness of Sally's racial and national liminality, the rebel admonishes her: "And you, Miss 'not Americaine': Remember. You stand for something." Scenes such as these, as well as Sally's facial expressions—which betray a con-

stant sense of anguish and fear—afford the production a greater
degree of complexity and ambivalence about the union. In another such scene, Jefferson acknowledges to Sally, "My head and
my heart wrestle with the consequences of this. You are too
young and too vulnerable and you are my . . . [y]ou are in my
service." In this dramatization, Jefferson is clearly cognizant of
the morally suspect nature of his position of dominion over
Sally's destiny, as well as his culpability in thwarting her emancipation. To some degree, this rendering constitutes a reworking
of the standard "tragic mulatto" plot, in which the white seducer
may be oblivious of or even remorseful about the mulatta's
sexual ruination, but he never raises serious questions about
her condition of absolute subservience. In antislavery fiction,
however, the very callousness of the planter in the face of the
mulatta's fate is meant to convey the overweening power the
Southern patriarch holds under slavery, whereas in *Sally Hemings*, Jefferson's ethical tribulations serve to enhance his identifi-
catory appeal as the benighted lover. Ultimately, both films
represent the founder as a morally conflicted and romantically
enraptured figure—and therefore one who is all the more engaging to viewers.

Still, even a muted interrogation of white supremacy and
racialized power appears to be too threatening for a network
television audience. Andrews writes that though she insisted that
Sally not become "some passive, inept slave with no purpose
other than the sexual pleasure for [*sic*] an influential white man
of power," the network rewrote key scenes in such a way as to
reproduce the stereotype in Sally of the black woman as sexually
provocative. For example, the first love scene was changed from
one in which the two principals were "drawn to each other"
to one in which Sally pulls off her gown, "sexually presenting
herself to a Jefferson standing at the door."[10] Such a spectacle
not only rehearses the stock figure of the mulatta as sexual
temptress but also bolsters the love-story imperative by

endorsing a nineteenth-century myth of willing black submission to white patriarchal authority. Unfortunately, Andrews herself participates in the romantic narrative of national origins to the extent that her vision of the Jefferson and Hemings association is intended to teach us that "perhaps for the same reason we cannot choose the people we're related to, alas, human nature dictates we cannot repel the feelings we have for people we're captivated by, either."[11] The verb chosen here is revealing for its rhetorical ability to suggest a political dimension while insisting primarily on a sense of mutual romantic "captivation." In this way, *Sally Hemings: An American Scandal*, like its predecessor, finally participates in a myth of American racial history that masks the workings of white supremacy under the cover of interracial romance.

THE WIND DONE GONE: THE ANTITRAGIC MULATTA TALE

If the above mass media reimaginings of the primal American racial scene do more to preserve the "tragic mulatta" as a figure of subjugation than they do to refute it, Alice Randall's *The Wind Done Gone* provides a contemporary, self-conscious recuperation of the figure that works from the resistant elements of antislavery fiction and augments them with twenty-first-century insights into the complex and ideological workings of race and nationalism. The recent best seller aims to place the mixed-race woman subject at the very center of "the birth of the nation," literally "coloring" the scene of U.S. racial history and domesticity through the vehicle of the iconic 1936 novel *Gone with the Wind*.

As with the ongoing dispute over the issue of Jefferson's progeny, the intensity of the legal battle over Randall's right to issue her parody signifies more than the judicial matter at hand—in this case a quarrel over copyright law. Rather, the conflict—like the Jefferson and Hemings affair—makes manifest the depth of the enduring contest over competing versions of America's racial past. The irregular nature of the resolution between the protectors of the Margaret Mitchell estate—which had tried to block the book's publication in 2001 on the grounds that it was a sequel rather than a parody—and Houghton Mifflin, which published the book while the case was still on appeal, evinces the racially charged essence of the case: in a settlement that could be regarded as a strategic public relations move, lawyers for the Mitchell trust agreed to drop its yearlong court challenge in return for an "unspecified contribution" by the publisher to Morehouse College, the historically black school in Atlanta.[12]

Such litigation would not have been necessary if Randall's parody had not been "a transformative work," as one legal commentator has claimed. Indeed, Jeffrey D. Grosset embellishes, "Randall's literary skewering of the inhabitants of Atlanta, Tara, and Twelve Oaks may well have dealt the sharpest blow to the antebellum South since Sherman's march to the sea."[13] At the center of this "literary skewering" is Cynara, Mammy's illegitimate mulatta daughter with "Planter," the counterpart to Gerald O'Hara, the plantation patriarch in the original work. The narrative perspective is Cynara's, and it is her "diary" that exposes the complexity of domestic life on the plantation. In Randall's revision, blacks occupy central stage rather than whites, and women over men. Also in *The Wind Done Gone*, Randall subverts the typical "tragic mulatta" narrative, in which the mixed-race slave is seduced and abandoned by a white planter. Instead, "R.," the Rhett Butler analogue, has to convince Cynara to marry him. When he kneels to propose, he is bereft of the power and glamour of the original. On the contrary, Cynara recounts, "He looked like what he was—a courtier from an age gone by. I found the effect of effort wed to feebleness endearing. Gallantry is never so visible as when it is doomed."[14] The marriage, which occurs during Reconstruction, is short-lived in the revised rendering. Reversing the tradition of mulatta fiction, Cynara soon abandons R. for a dashing black congressman, with whom she has a child.

In interviews, Randall herself has explained that "the central act of my parody is to give Mammy a child, and to give that child a voice." She describes Cynara as a "not-so-tragic mulatto" who "reads and writes her way into being."[15] Cynara achieves this agency through an unmasking of the romantic and segregated domestic fantasy that undergirds the culturally formative *Gone with the Wind*. Randall's parody reveals a plantation world in which interracial intimacy is taken for granted in multiform dimensions made invisible in its literary predecessor. For example, cross-racial mother love is a predominant theme in *The Wind Done Gone* and an integral component of life on "Tata," Randall's loaded term for the original "Tara." While Mammy serves as wet nurse to "Other" (Cynara's half-sister and the counterpart to Mitchell's Scarlett), "Lady," Other's mother, herself envious of Mammy's maternal attentions, gratifies her longing by nursing Cynara: "She pulled me to her lap and I suckled at her breast till her warm milk filled me. As always, it was a cheering surprise for both of us. We had been sharing these little spurred-by-envy suppers all my memory, but each time the milk came and how long it came without running out was a mystery to us both. Later, when I slept beside her, she said, 'You're my little girl, aren't you?'" In fact, Cynara and Other exchange the maternal breast to such an extent that Cynara later exclaims, "When it comes right down to it, I am Lady's child and she is Mammy's."[16] On "Tata," then, when it comes to maternal intimacy, conventional racial associations become utterly blurred and intersecting. At one point, Cynara describes these intricate familial workings in comparing "the truth of body" with "the truth of soul": "Planter slept with Mammy in pleasure all their lives. In truth of body, I was the real passion fruit, and Other was the bloom of civil rape. In truth of soul, Other was raised in the humidity of desire suckling boldly at Mammy's breast, and I was raised in the cool restraint of Lady's boudoir, the place to which you retreat with dignity, a place of private sorrows and private consolations, the touch of Lady's soft hand lavished on my hapless head. So Other was a child of pleasure and I a child of cold chastity, willing to be bred."[17]

One effect of this scene of Cynara's relative asceticism is to challenge and supercede the abiding image of the sexually rapacious black woman. A broader effect of Randall's work is to rescue the Mammy figure from the oblivion of earlier "tragic mulatto" portrayals. Instead, *The Wind Done Gone* suggests, the story of antebellum race history is the story of enduring mother love in a complicated configuration of black and white permutations. Moreover, this sense of fluid maternal boundaries in *The Wind Done Gone* extends to the racial origins of Lady and Other, whom we learn are both of mixed descent. Lady's great-grandmother, it turns out, was a Haitian "negress."

Furthermore, while the notion of race is meaningless for Cynara as a proportion of blood, it nonetheless holds another kind of powerful and profound significance: "It is not in the pigment of my skin that my negressness lies. It is not the color of my skin. It is the color of my mind, and my mind is dark, dusky, like a beautiful night. And Other, my part-sister, had the dusky blood but not the mind, not the memory."[18] Here, Randall self-consciously invokes contemporary understandings about the constructed nature of race, superimposing them onto her antebellum characters to illustrate the importance of such categories as shared "mind," "memory," and history in delineating cultural affinities. With this sociocultural definition of racial identity, *The Wind Done Gone* distinguishes itself conspicuously from the tradition of miscegenation fiction in general and the "tragic mulatto" genre in particular, in that rigid racial demarcations are vital to their narrative premises. The demarcation and transgression of essential racial classifications form the cornerstone for such stories. In Randall's novel, by contrast, race as a matter of biology is always already confounded. It is as if, for Randall, everyone is a "tragic mulatto." Or if so, then no one is. In one scene, Cynara's congressman suitor exclaims: "Until it is transformed by our own energy, our own muscle, our own brain, every second of our existence on these shores is tragic. . . . And once transformed, *even the least little bit*, one drop of transformation, in the entire body of a life, makes the life victorious."[19] In this way, the congressman employs the metaphor of scientific racism and the "one-drop rule" to frustrate and undo its effects. In his view, a resistant "tragic mulatta" is a "victorious" one.

Thus, Randall's parody echoes the proposition implied but never credited in many of the nineteenth-century antislavery writings in this study: that far from a figure worthy of derision, the mulatta constitutes the quintessential American in her racial hybridity. More than that, just as the congressman called upon Cynara individually to reconceive of her subjugated status, so, too, can we view the body of "tragic mulatto" fiction in its entirety as constituting its own "victory" over received racial doctrine and official conceptions of the American self. Presaging Randall and working within their historical and cultural constraints, abolitionist writers deployed the mulatta exemplar to mount similar interrogations into existing hierarchies of identity at the crossroads of race and nation. In other words, 150 years before critical race theory made a novel like *The Wind Done Gone* possible, writers in the "tragic mulatta" tradition were successfully scrutinizing the intricate and interpenetrated workings of racial and national personhood.

Notes

Introduction: Reading Miscegenation

1. In the journalistic arena, examples include a full issue of *Newsweek* devoted to "Redefining Race in America"; such newspaper articles as Vanessa E. Jones, "A Rich Sense of Self"; and Lisa Jones, "Are We Tiger Woods Yet?" Lisa Jones makes the point that the "Tiger Woods phenomenon" can be characterized more as "image equity"—a corporate-sponsored "illusion of change"—than any representation of substantive social progress. In terms of literary illustrations of a renewed focus on interracialism, see James McBride, *The Color of Water*; Danzy Senna, *Caucasia*; Shirlee Taylor Haizlip, *The Sweeter the Juice*; Lise Funderburg, *Black, White, Other*.

2. The decision to allow respondents to check off more than one box was a compromise reached after the idea of including a "multiracial" category met with vociferous resistance from various constituencies. The result meant that, from a governmental standpoint at least, multiracial people did not exist. See Tatsha Robertson, "Minorities Fear Census Falls Short"; Cindy Rodriguez, "Civil Rights Groups Wary of Census Data on Race." See also Sarah Chinn's excellent discussion of this controversy in *Technology and the Logic of American Racism*.

3. The Compromise of 1850 admitted California as a free state, allowed for popular sovereignty when the Utah and New Mexico territories applied for statehood, enacted the infamous fugitive slave law of 1850, and abolished the slave trade in the District of Columbia. See Michael F. Holt, *The Political Crisis of the 1850s*, 68.

4. Margo J. Anderson, *The American Census*. See also Margo J. Anderson and Stephen E. Fienberg, eds., *Who Counts?* 20–23.

5. Qtd. in Reginald Horsman, *Race and Manifest Destiny*, 282.

6. See Elise Lemire, *"Miscegenation."* Lemire argues that "'amalgamation' and 'miscegenation' were terms that did the work of enforcing the prohibition against certain marriages, such that social and economic equality would not follow the granting of any black political rights, and thereby making whiteness a category of people with certain sexual race preferences, all without seeming prejudicial due to the insistence implicit in the terms on [*sic*] the biological real" (4).

7. Joel Williamson, *New People*, 75.
8. Scott L. Malcolmson, *One Drop of Blood*, 198.
9. Mary Grant, *North Over South*, 33.
10. Eva Saks, "Representing Miscegenation Law," 42.
11. See Sidney Kaplan, "The Miscegenation Issue in the Election of 1864," 47–100. See also George M. Fredrickson, *The Black Image in the White Mind*, 171–172. For a discussion of the political scandal and contemporaneous racial anxiety, see Eve Allegra Raimon, "*Miscegenation*, 'Melaleukation' and Public Reception," 121–132. Though it is technically anachronistic, for clarity's sake I will typically employ the more familiar "miscegenation" rather than "amalgamation."
12. Sterling Brown, *The Negro in American Fiction*, 144, qtd. in Judith R. Berzon, *Neither White Nor Black*, 100.
13. Berzon, *Neither White Nor Black*, 100.
14. Werner Sollors, *Neither Black Nor White Yet Both*, 127–128.
15. Jennifer DeVere Brody, *Impossible Purities*, 16. Using visual, theatrical, and literary texts, Brody's project is to demonstrate how " 'black' (racialized and sexualized) women were indispensable to the construction of Englishness as a new form of 'white' male subjectivity" (7).
16. To Berzon, the exemplar is defined as "the almost-white character whose beauty, intelligence, and purity are forever in conflict with the 'savage primitivism' inherited from his or her Negro ancestry." See *Neither White Nor Black*, 99.
17. Nina Baym, *Woman's Fiction*, 35.
18. Sollors, *Neither Black Nor White Yet Both*, 222–223.
19. Malcolmson, *One Drop of Blood*, 218. The emphasis on the reproductive potential of mulattas is as crucial to the tradition as is their relative sexual powerlessness. Her male counterparts, on the other hand, are distinguished by their comparative strength and authority. George Harris in *Uncle Tom's Cabin* is perhaps the most famous example of this alternative masculine tradition. Richard Yarborough compares the "rational," "articulate" Harris with Tom, his "passive," "simple," "full-blood" counterpart. Yarborough remarks about the pairing: "A full-blood Clark Kent and a mulatto Superman, they are never on stage at the same time." See "Strategies of Black Characterization," 53.
20. Ann duCille notes that "Clotel has been more dismissed and maligned than studied and mined" ("Where in the World Is William Wells Brown?" 453).
21. Jean Fagan Yellin, *Women and Sisters*, 73.
22. Carolyn L. Karcher, "Rape, Murder, Revenge in 'Slavery's Pleasant Homes,' " 330. For classic elaborations of this view, see, for example, Barbara Christian, *Black Women Novelists*; Karen Sánchez-Eppler, "Bodily Bonds"; Arlene A. Elder, *"Hindered Hand."*
23. Malcolmson, *One Drop of Blood*, 218.

24. Ann duCille, *The Coupling Convention*, 7.
25. duCille, "Where in the World Is William Wells Brown?" 454.
26. Wai-Chee Dimock, "Feminism, New Historicism, and the Reader," 601.
27. Hazel V. Carby, *Reconstructing Womanhood*, 89, emphasis added. I extend the discussion to white authors as well, not because I see the aims of both as identical but because up to now critics have focused on the figure's constraining rather than enabling properties.
28. Etienne Balibar and Immanel Wallerstein, *Race, Nation, Class*, 76.
29. For a discussion of the journalistic controversy in which Jefferson was first accused of having coupled with an "African Venus concubine" to produce "sable" children of "African stock," see Lemire, *"Miscegenation,"* 11–34. Lemire contends that the discourse the controversy engendered helped to reify and biologize notions that we now know of as "intraracial" and "interracial" desire. She writes that "in the wake of a state-sanctioned philosophy of equality, intraracial desire was an important means of maintaining a race-based culture, not because mixed-race people would otherwise result—although this was raised as a concern at times—but because it proved one's affiliation to the idea of white superiority and thus to whiteness itself" (33–34).
30. William Wells Brown, *Clotel*, 246.
31. Harriet Wilson, *Our Nig*.
32. The question of which novel holds the distinction of the earliest to be written by an African American woman is now complicated by the appearance of Hannah Crafts's *The Bondwoman's Narrative*, the second work after *Our Nig* to be recovered under the auspices of Henry Louis Gates Jr.
33. Amy Kaplan has recently pointed out that "scholars have overlooked the fact that the development of domestic discourse in America is contemporaneous with the discourse of Manifest Destiny" ("Manifest Domesticity," 583).
34. From the introduction to *The Slave; or, Memoirs of Archy Moore* by "F.C.S." in a reprint of the original edition, edited by Clarence Ghodes, n.p. The volume is part of a series of "American Novels of Muckraking, Propaganda, and Social Protest." According to this introduction, John H. Eastburn, the novel's original printer and the official printer for the city of Boston, lost his job after the book appeared.
35. Carolyn L. Karcher, *The First Woman of the Republic*, 343.
36. Sánchez-Eppler, "Bodily Bonds," 29.
37. Jules Zanger was one of the earliest critics to articulate the work the "tragic mulatto" performed to advance cross-racial lines of identification based on gender solidarity. In 1966, he contended that since antebellum white women were as dependent on their husbands as "the poor octoroon" was upon her slave master/father, the anti-

slavery writer "could draw upon the audience's own dread of the life they would face if the bank failed, the tariff were defeated, the speculation fizzled." See "The Tragic Octoroon in Pre–Civil War Fiction," 67. Granted Zanger overemphasizes class and gender considerations as compared with racial difference, but by the same token later commentators have gone too far in discounting the figure's agency as well as the politically powerful potential in narrative strategies of identification.

38. Sterling Brown, *Negro Poetry and Drama* (1937), reprinted in *The Negro in American Fiction*, 133.

39. Jane Tompkins, *Sensational Designs*. As Mason Stokes makes clear in *The Color of Sex*, Tompkins's book was responsible for changing the course of literary studies for arguing that a text's popularity in and of itself justifies critical inquiry and for her insistence that aesthetic judgment has a history that has been shaped by modernist criteria. See *The Color of Sex*, 8. For an example of a critical analysis of the "tragic mulatto" that is congruous with Tompkins's view, see Susan Gilman, "The Mulatto, Tragic or Triumphant?" 221–243.

40. Lauren Berlant, "Poor Eliza," 641.

41. Gilman, "The Mulatto," 225.

42. Dana Nelson, *The Word in Black and White*, xii.

43. Stokes, *The Color of Sex*, 5. Stokes argues that in plantation fiction, the responsibility for upholding "racial purity" fell on plantation mistresses rather than on the planters themselves. Furthermore, "any threat to that purity got transmuted, through the energies of patriarchy, into a threat against white men, who then found it even more necessary to shore up the franchise of whiteness." That is to say that "whiteness insists on female purity, but it only really appears in the absence of that purity" (35).

44. Chinn, *Technology and the Logic of American Racism*, xiv.

45. Lydia Maria Child, "Willie Wharton," 324–345; Child, *A Romance of the Republic*.

46. Brown, *Clotel*, 145–148, 174–181.

47. Eric Sundquist, ed., *New Essays on* Uncle Tom's Cabin, 16–17. Sundquist adds that *The Slave* "offers a number of potential parallels in plot and character to *Uncle Tom's Cabin* that are, if anything, watered down and undermined by Stowe" (17).

48. Robert B. Stepto, "Sharing the Thunder," 136.

49. F.C.S., introduction to *The Slave*, n.p. Jean Fagan Yellin has concluded that next to Hildreth's work, "the only other antislavery novel with comparable force is Uncle Tom's Cabin" (*The Intricate Knot*, 85).

50. Richard Hildreth, *The Slave*, 1:54.

51. Werner Sollors has noted in this connection that "in reading the literature on the Tragic Mulatto it is . . . striking to find that the text in front of us only rarely seems to fit the stereotype that it supposedly

so rigidly and unchangingly and ineluctably embodies" (*Neither White Nor Black Yet Both*, 238).

52. Harriet Beecher Stowe, *Uncle Tom's Cabin*, 608. Here, I follow Gillian Brown's argument that the family's exit to Liberia allows Stowe to "do away with blackness, the mark of incongruity and exogamy" (*Domestic Individualism*, 59).

53. Alice Randall, *The Wind Done Gone*; *Jefferson in Paris*, dir. James Ivory, Touchstone Pictures, 1995; *Sally Hemings: An American Scandal*, dir. Charles Haid, Artisan Productions, 2000.

54. Rita Felski, *The Gender of Modernity*, 142.

55. Ann Cvetkovich, *Mixed Feelings*, 38.

Chapter 1 Of Romances and Republics in Lydia Maria Child's Miscegenation Fiction

1. Carolyn L. Karcher, *A Lydia Maria Child Reader*, 3.

2. Victor Sejour's short story "Le Mulatre" (1837) is often afforded originary status in the tradition. Another early example is John Gabriel Stedman's *Narrative of Joanna* (1838).

3. Yellin, *Women and Sisters*, 71.

4. Maggie Sale, "Critiques from Within," 696–718.

5. Horsman, *Race and Manifest Destiny*, 100. Horsman notes that "long before scientists and others developed an intellectual rationale to justify the permanent inferiority of nonwhites, the process of debasing blacks had been carried out in the daily life of America, and, whatever the theory, blacks in practice were not regarded merely as men and women of a different complexion" (100).

6. Horsman, *Race and Manifest Destiny*, 23.

7. John O'Sullivan, qtd. in Anders Stephanson, *Manifest Destiny*, 44–45.

8. Qtd. in Horsman, *Race and Manifest Destiny*, 130.

9. Malcolmson, *One Drop of Blood*, 210.

10. Rachel F. Moran, *Interracial Intimacy*, 25.

11. Williamson, *New People*, 67, 73.

12. Carby, *Reconstructing Womanhood*, 89. Carby offers this insight in connection with a discussion of Frances E. W. Harper's *Iola Leroy* (1892), but it is equally germane in this context.

13. Karcher, *The First Woman of the Republic*, 20. Karcher notes that *Hobomok* is based on the narrative poem "Yamoyden, A Tale of the Wars of King Philip, in Six Cantos," by James Wallis Eastburn and Robert Sands (1820). Child had earlier discovered an appreciation of the poem in the *North American Review*. The essay praised the poem for making use of the "unequaled fitness of our early history for the purposes of a work of fiction" (Karcher, *The First Woman of the Republic*, 20).

14. Child, *Hobomok*, 7.

15. For an example of an analysis that concentrates almost exclusively

on the issue of miscegenation, see Deborah Pickman Clifford, *Crusader for Freedom*, 42–45; see also the introduction to Carolyn L. Karcher, ed., *Hobomok and Other Writings on Indians*. Karcher offers a detailed analysis of the religious and feminist dimensions of the novel as well in *The First Woman of the Republic*.

16. Lydia Maria Child, *Hobomok*, 65.
17. Karcher, *The First Woman of the Republic*, 10–11.
18. Later in her career, Child would reject even Swedenborgianism for its doctrinal rigidity, yet she would carry over its basic optimism in her adherence to the more socially conscious views of the radical social scientist Charles Fourier. Fourier believed that "faulty social organization" was to blame for society's ills and that it was possible to construct a "perfect order" based on "the laws of harmony" by "rearranging economic relationships." See Ann C. Rose, *Transcendentalism as a Social Movement*, 141.
19. For a discussion of Child's antebellum nonpartisanship, see Margaret R. Kellow, "Duties Are Ours," 32–33. Kellow asserts that prior to the Compromise of 1850, Child maintained that "slavery was pre-eminently a moral problem" and that partisan politics was "more likely to obstruct than to accelerate" the moral transformation necessary among slaveholders. Northern compliance with the Fugitive Slave Act, as well as the South's determination to frustrate settlement of the new western territories with free-state emigrants, helped persuade her, ultimately, to support the Republican candidacy of John C. Frémont.
20. Child, *Hobomok*, 133.
21. Ibid., 133, 135.
22. Ibid., 135.
23. Lydia Maria Child to Theodore Dwight Weld, March 7, 1839, *Selected Letters*, 104–105.
24. Lydia Maria Child to Lucy Larcom, March 12, 1873, *Selected Letters*, 511.
25. Child, *Hobomok*, 137, 150.
26. Review of *Hobomok* in *North American Review* 19 (July 1824): 263.
27. Clifford, *Crusader for Freedom*, 44–45; Karcher, *The First Woman of the Republic*, 38–39.
28. Karcher, *The First Woman of the Republic*, 37.
29. Lydia Maria Child, *An Appeal in Favor of That Class of Americans Called Africans*, 187.
30. Ibid., 126, 125.
31. Ibid., 22.
32. Ibid., preface.
33. Karcher, *The First Woman of the Republic*, 192.
34. "Mrs. Child's 'Appeal,'" reprinted in the *Liberator*, December 14, 1833, 200.
35. Bruce Mills, *Cultural Reformations*, 31–32.

36. Lydia Maria Child to Maria Weston Chapman, May 11, 1842, *Selected Letters*, 175.
37. Lydia Maria Child to Francis Shaw, February 15, 1842, *Selected Letters*, 161; Child to James Miller McKim, *Selected Letters*, January 26, 1842, 158.
38. Karcher, "Rape, Murder, and Revenge," 331.
39. Bruce Mills, "Lydia Maria Child and the Endings to Harriet Jacobs' *Incidents in the Life of a Slave Girl*," 255–271.
40. Saks, "Representing Miscegenation Law," 64.
41. William L. Andrews, "Inter(racial)textuality in Nineteenth-Century Southern Narrative," 304.
42. Lydia Maria Child, "Slavery's Pleasant Homes," 148.
43. Ibid., 148–149
44. In "The Flower of Black Female Sexuality in Pauline Hopkins's *Winona*," Dorri Rabung Beam notes the common tendency for flower imagery to suggest black female sexuality in African American women's fiction. She argues that Hopkins "appropriates flower language to describe her own black heroine and to critique racist distinctions between a delicate white female body and a fleshly sexualized black female body" (80).
45. Saks, "Representing Miscegenation Law," 64.
46. I refer, of course, to the relentless sexual intimidation of the protagonist, Linda Brent, by her master, Dr. Flint.
47. Child, "Slavery's Pleasant Homes," 152–153, 156.
48. Ibid., 160.
49. Child, "Willie Wharton," 325.
50. Ibid.
51. Ibid., 325–327.
52. Ibid., 333, 334.
53. Ibid., 337.
54. Ibid., 342.
55. Ibid., 343.
56. Clifford, *Crusader for Freedom*, 285.
57. Child, "Willie Wharton," 343.
58. Ibid., 343, 344.
59. Christopher Castiglia, *Bound and Determined*, 7.
60. Child, "Willie Wharton," 345.
61. Ibid.
62. Lydia Maria Child to Robert Purvis, August 14, 1868, *Selected Letters*, 482–483.
63. Clifford, *Crusader for Freedom*, 272–274.
64. Lydia Maria Child to Francis Shaw, October 1846, *Selected Letters*, 230.
65. Eric Foner, *Reconstruction*, 156.
66. Child, *An Appeal*, 212.
67. Foner, *Reconstruction*, 158.

68. Lydia Maria Child, "Through the Red Sea into the Wilderness," *Independent*, December 21, 1865, 1, reprinted in the *Liberator*, December 29, 1865, 205. Before becoming so disillusioned with Johnson, Child had recounted in an 1864 letter that black crowds in Nashville had called to him, "You are our Moses." See Lydia Maria Child to John Fraser, November 10, 1964, *Selected Letters*, 449. Karcher uses this passage from the *Liberator* article as an epigraph for her chapter on *A Romance of the Republic* in *The First Woman in the Republic*.

69. In advocating interracial marriage, Child also takes aim at the proprietary aspects of the marriage institution itself regardless of race. Karcher observes that "whatever the defects of the marriage plot as a vehicle for Child's egalitarian precepts, it did lead her to brilliant insights into the complex relationship between the racial slave system that victimized African Americans and the patriarchal system that victimized women" (*The First Woman of the Republic*, 514).

70. Child, *A Romance of the Republic*, 102.

71. Lydia Maria Child to William P. Cutler, July 10, 1862, *Selected Letters*, 414.

72. Child, *A Romance of the Republic*, 302.

73. Ibid., 432.

74. Ibid., 382–383.

75. Ibid., 380.

76. Ibid., 390.

77. Teresa Zackodnik notes that Virginia was the first colony to adopt an antimiscegenation law in 1662 and that such statutes marked a clear departure from the long-standing English law of patriarchal descent. Since Virginia's version first applied to "all children born in the country," however, it required revision since it failed to take into account the status of children born to white mothers and black fathers. See "Fixing the Color Line," 420–451.

78. Child, *A Romance of the Republic*, 440.

79. Dana Nelson has written in this connection that this seeming withdrawal from prior challenges in the novel to established hierarchies of race can be attributed to Child's failure to allow "a positive evaluation of cultural or social configurations different from those of the white middle class." See *The Word in Black and White*, 88.

CHAPTER 2 REVISING THE "QUADROON NARRATIVE" IN WILLIAM WELLS BROWN'S *CLOTEL*

1. See Kaplan, "The Miscegenation Issue," 47–100. See also Fredrickson, *The Black Image in the White Mind*, 171–172. For a discussion of the political scandal and contemporaneous racial anxiety, see Raimon, "*Miscegenation*, 'Melaleukation' and Public Reception," 121–132.

2. Though Peterson's focus is on female writers, the same observation holds for male authors. See Carla L. Peterson, *"Doers of the Word,"* 149.

3. For purposes of clarity and since it is the original, I will confine my comments to this version of the novel rather than the two later revisions, entitled *Miralda; or, The Beautiful Quadroon* and *Clotelle; or, The Colored Heroine.* For a useful comparison of the different versions, see Yellin, *The Intricate Knot,* 174–177.

4. Brown, *Clotel,* 245.

5. Child, "The Quadroons," 3. It is noteworthy that in these passages, "reality" to the female protagonist is defined as precisely what is legally proscribed in the social sphere, signaling literature's mediated relation to "the real."

6. Brown, *Clotel,* 245, 84.

7. Child, "The Quadroons," 4. Carolyn L. Karcher points to Brown's "plagiarism" of these passages to suggest his "discomfort with the tragic mulatto theme." She further asserts that Brown "borrows Child's description of the refined mulatto heroine precisely because it conveys a white view of his own people that he does not share and therefore cannot articulate for himself." Setting aside the rhetorical, instrumental dimension of Brown's use of the figure, Karcher's assessment suggests that Brown lacked the ability to create a suitable replacement for Child's narrative model. See "Lydia Maria Child's *Romance of the Republic,*" 101n.6.

8. William Edward Farrison, *William Wells Brown,* 9–10. For a useful survey of studies concerning Jefferson's reputed sexual relations with his slave Sally Hemings, see B. R. Burg, "The Rhetoric of Miscegenation," 128–138. See also Fawn M. Brodie, *Thomas Jefferson.* Brodie was among the first historians to argue that the charges, which first surfaced in a series of articles in the *Richmond (Virginia) Recorder* in 1802, were substantially true.

9. On Jefferson's paternity, see Brian Duffy, "Jefferson's Secret Life," 58. For an examination of the racial politics surrounding the controversy, see Annette Gordon-Reed, "Engaging Jefferson," 171–182.

10. duCille, "Where in the World Is William Wells Brown?" 451.

11. Brown, *Clotel,* 16.

12. Ibid., 246.

13. I refer here to the tradition that begins with Child and continues through the writings of such diverse authors as Harriet Beecher Stowe, Charles Chestnutt, George Washington Cable, Mark Twain, Pauline Hopkins, and Nella Larson, to name a handful.

14. Vernon Loggins, *The Negro Author,* 166.

15. William L. Andrews, "The Novelization of Voice in Early African Narrative," 23–34.

16. Andrews borrows this term from Barbara Hernnstein Smith, who defines "natural discourse" as "the verbal acts of real persons on

particular occasions in response to particular sets of circumstances."
See Smith, *On the Margins of Discourse*, 21–22.

17. Andrews, "The Novelization of Voice," 31.
18. At the same time, Brown's emphasis on the interracial origins of American national mythology suggests that he does not want to reject race as a meaningful signifier. This tension is implicit throughout *Clotel*, though never addressed directly.
19. Brown, *Clotel*, 59.
20. I am indebted to Phillip Brian Harper for this insight concerning the workings of negative identification in *Clotel*.
21. Joel Williamson writes in this connection that "the organic society of the Old South found an important part of its strength in the dichotomous nature of western civilization. Opposites were held in tight tension in the organic society—slavery was set against freedom, white against black, and men were strenuously balanced by women. Increasingly, the South grew furiously intolerant of anything that was not distinctly slave or free, black or white, male or female" (*New People*, 74).
22. Brown, *Clotel*, 63.
23. Andrews, "The Novelization of Voice," 32.
24. Brown, *Clotel*, 66.
25. Carby, *Reconstructing Womanhood*, 89.
26. Shirley Samuels, ed., *The Culture of Sentiment*, 3.
27. Karen Sánchez-Eppler, *Touching Liberty*, 1. Sánchez-Eppler goes on to point out that, with the enactment of the Fourteenth and Fifteenth Amendments, the focus shifted from corporeal oppression to juridical exclusion, with the ironic result that "in focusing on suffrage, these movements of social protest came to reiterate the rhetoric of abstract personhood that had traditionally erased and silenced their distinct flesh" (5).
28. Brown, *Clotel,* 66
29. Ibid., 178.
30. Richard H. Sewell, *Ballots for Freedom*, 142. Pennsylvania Democrat David Wilmot offered a proviso to an 1846 bill proclaiming that slavery should be banned in the territories acquired from Mexico. See Samuel Eliot Morison and Henry Steel Commager, *The Growth of the American Republic*, 471–474. Far from conceiving of it as a problack measure, Wilmot himself called it the "White Man's Proviso" and told the House that barring slavery from the Mexican territories would safeguard the region for 'the sons of toil, of my own race and color.'" See Eric Foner, *Free Soil, Free Labor, Free Men*, 267.
31. Brown, *Clotel*, 179.
32. I am indebted to Jean Fagan Yellin for referring me to Webster's "Seventh of March" speech. See Morison and Commager, *The Growth of the American Republic*, 478. For a discussion of Webster's support of African colonization, see Foner, *Free Soil,* 268.

33. Brown, *Clotel*, 179–180.
34. David A. Gerber, *Black Ohio and the Color Line*, 8.
35. Leon F. Litwack, *North of Slavery*, 64–112.
36. See Melissa Nobles, *Shades of Citizenship*.
37. Brown, *Clotel*, 172.
38. Ibid., 174.
39. Benjamin Quarles, *Black Abolitionists*, 63.
40. Brown, *Clotel*, 194.
41. Ibid., 172, 194, 204.
42. Marjorie Garber, *Vested Interests*, 274. To Garber, "transvestism" in-cludes but is not limited to the "full gender-masquerade" of Brown's characters (275). I agree with her argument that "the possibility of crossing racial boundaries stirs fears of the possibility of crossing the boundaries of gender, and vice versa." However, her assertion that "what the 'black transvestite' does is to realize the latent dream thoughts—or nightmares—of American cultural mythology" (274) is troubling in that it lacks the historical specificity that would ac-count for changing cultural responses over time.
43. Brown, *Clotel*, 224, 227, 228.
44. Farrison, *William Wells Brown*, 228, x.
45. Brown, *Clotel*, 216.
46. Ibid., 216, 219.
47. Ibid., 219–220.
48. Ibid., 244.
49. Farrison, *William Wells Brown*, 197–246.
50. Brown, *Clotel*, 246.
51. Qtd. in Yellin, *The Intricate Knot*, 170.
52. Child, *A Romance of the Republic*, 440.

CHAPTER 3 RESISTANT CASSYS IN RICHARD HILDRETH'S
THE SLAVE AND HARRIET BEECHER STOWE'S
UNCLE TOM'S CABIN

1. Tompkins, *Sensational Designs*, 122. Tompkins's assessment is typical of a host of other summaries of the novel's literary-historical signif-icance. Richard Yarborough, for example, who finds the characters in *Uncle Tom's Cabin* "derivative" and "distorting," nevertheless con-cludes that "Stowe's work played a major role in establishing the level of discourse for the majority of fictional treatments of the Afro-American that were to follow—even for those produced by blacks themselves" ("Strategies of Black Characterization," 46). On a similar, if more affirmative note, Harryette Mullen proclaims that "*Uncle Tom's Cabin* can be regarded as an important precursor of the African American novel. Throughout the broad influence of this fic-tional work, Stowe almost single-handedly turned the interests of black readers and writers to the political, cultural, and economic

possibilities of the novel" ("Runaway Tongue," 244). Additionally, from a specifically feminist perspective, Elizabeth Ammons has argued that "it is impossible to overemphasize" the importance of the fact that it was a woman writer who issued "the most widely praised, widely read, widely sold American novel of the nineteenth century" ("Stowe's Dream of the Mother-Savior," 155).

2. Saks, "Representing Miscegenation Law," 42. For perhaps the fullest discussion of Stowe's complicity in hegemonic structures of power, see Brown, *Domestic Individualism*.

3. Before she began serializing *Uncle Tom's Cabin*, Stowe had already published a response to the Fugitive Slave Act in the *National Era* on August 1, 1850. "The Freeman's Dream," a parable, describes the consequences at judgment day for a farmer who refuses to help a family of fugitive slaves out of fear of defying the new law. Her famous declaration, "I will write something. I will if I live," occurs in response to a letter written by Isabella Beecher detailing the consequences of the act from her perspective in Boston. See Joan Hedrick, *Harriet Beecher Stowe*, 206–207.

4. Anderson, *The American Census*. See also Anderson and Fienberg, *Who Counts?* 20–23.

5. Nobles, *Shades of Citizenship*, 25–84.

6. Here, I refer, of course, to the growing predominance of the one-drop rule at midcentury in areas other than the Chesapeake and Louisiana. See James F. Davis, *Who Is Black*, 123–132, 137–139. See also Malcolmson, *One Drop of Blood*.

7. Williamson, *New People*, 24, 27, 58.

8. Ibid., 59.

9. George M. Fredrickson, *White Supremacy*. The element of arbitrariness in such efforts at racial classification is underscored in an 1835 court ruling, cited by Fredrickson, which concludes that it could not determine what "admixture . . . will make a colored person. . . . The condition is not to be determined solely by visible mixture . . . but by reputation" (120).

10. Winthrop D. Jordan, *White Over Black*, 178.

11. Ian Haney Lopez, *White by Law*, 10. See also Cheryl I. Harris, "Whiteness as Property," and other essays in Kimberle Crenshaw, Neil Gotenda, Gary Peller, and Kendall Thomas, eds., *Critical Race Theory*.

12. In this case, which established the freedom of Nanny Pagee and her children, the supreme court of Virginia declared that racial appearance should determine who bore the burden of proof in freedom suits. The court ruled that it was "incumbent of the defendant to have proved, if he could, that the plaintiff was descended in the maternal line from a slave." See A. Leon Higginbotham Jr. and Barbara K. Kopytoff, "Racial Purity and Interracial Sex in the Law in Colonial and Antebellum Virginia," 81.

13. Saks, "Representing Miscegenation Law," 67.
14. A sizable number of such middle-class white women—many of them Northerners—were themselves participants in abolitionist politics and either supported or contributed to such antislavery gift-books as the *Liberty Bell*, edited by Maria Weston Chapman and published by the Boston Anti-Slavery Society. The Scottish émigré Fanny Wright, who edited the weekly *Free Enquirer*, is another notable example, along with Child and feminist-abolitionist Amy Post.
15. Ronald T. Takaki, *Iron Cages*, 115.
16. See Brown, *Domestic Individualism*. For another discussion of Stowe's colonizationist views, see Yarborough, "Strategies of Black Characterization," 69–71.
17. Mullen, "Runaway Tongue," 244, emphasis added.
18. Other examples of this preexisting tradition, largely European in origin, include Gustave de Beaumont's *Marie* (1835), Dion Boucicault's play *The Octoroon* (1859), and Joseph Holt Ingraham's novel *The Quadroone; or, St. Michael's Day* (1841). See Sollors, *Neither Black Nor White Yet Both*, 112–141, 220–245.
19. Among the personal experiences Stowe apparently drew from in writing *Uncle Tom's Cabin* was an incident involving an unnamed servant who had been employed by the Stowe family during their years in Cincinnati. A few months after the woman began working for them, according to the story, Calvin Stowe, Harriet's husband, received word that the fugitive's master was searching the city for her. Joan Hedrick's biography recounts the events that supposedly followed: "Calvin Stowe and Henry Ward Beecher armed themselves and drove the woman twelve miles by back roads to John Van Zandt's cabin, a station on the Underground Railroad." See *Harriet Beecher Stowe*, 121. The incident is supposed to have inspired Stowe to write the story of Eliza's escape. For a discussion of the contradictory nature of the sources for this episode, see E. Bruce Kirkham, *The Building of Uncle Tom's Cabin*, 104–112.
20. Harriet Beecher Stowe, *The Key to Uncle Tom's Cabin*, 13–14.
21. Catherine E. O'Connell invokes Michael Bakhtin's term "heteroglossia" in connection with *Uncle Tom's Cabin* to capture the sense that the novel "contains so many social languages in competition or dialogue with each other." See " 'The Magic of the Real Presence of Distress,' " n.1.
22. Yellin's *The Intricate Knot*, which appeared more than thirty years ago, constitutes one of the few exceptions to this tradition of critical oversight of Hildreth's novel. Yellin's focus, however, is on the literary history surrounding the book as opposed to providing a sustained critical analysis.
23. Yellin notes that "the single most remarkable thing about *The Slave* is this first-person narration: the Boston attorney has assumed the identity of a plantation slave. The book's acceptance as autobiography

has been so complete that it has been discredited as a false slave narrative; even twentieth-century critics have felt it necessary to point out that it is fiction" (*The Intricate Knot,* 92).

24. Yellin, *The Intricate Knot*, 91.
25. John M. Werner, *Reaping the Bloody Harvest*, 286–287.
26. A second version appeared in 1852 after the runaway success of Stowe's novel that was retitled *The White Slave; or, Memoirs of a Fugitive*. In an 1855 edition, Hildreth recounts the original's translation into French, Italian, and German and maintains the work's status as "the first successful application of fictitious narrative to anti-slavery purposes" (xxi).
27. Qtd. in Yellin, *The Intricate Knot*, 101.
28. Qtd. in Yellin, *The Intricate Knot*, 101–102.
29. F.C.S., *The Slave*, n.p.
30. Yarborough, "Strategies of Black Characterization," 75.
31. Hildreth, *The Slave*, 1:4.
32. Ibid., 1:5, 6.
33. Ibid., 1:6.
34. Saks, "Representing Miscegenation Law," 53–54.
35. Hildreth, *The Slave*, 1:27–28.
36. Ibid., 1:41.
37. The comic characters of Andy and "Black Sam," who is "three shades darker than any other son of ebony on the place" (95), are two such examples of class stratification in *Uncle Tom's Cabin*. Sambo and Quimbo, with their "coarse, dark, heavy features" and their "barbarous, guttural, half-brute intonation" (493), are also representative. It is characteristic for such characters to speak in heavy dialect.
38. Hildreth, *The Slave*, 1:41–42.
39. Ibid., 1:48–49.
40. Ibid., 1:54.
41. Richard Hildreth, *Despotism in America*, 36–38.
42. Hildreth, *The Slave*, 2:9.
43. Ibid., 2:49–50.
44. Ibid., 2:51.
45. Hildreth, *Despotism in America*, 35–38.
46. Hildreth, *The Slave*, 2:72, 94.
47. Ibid., 2:117.
48. Stowe, *Uncle Tom's Cabin*, 515–516, 517, 518.
49. Ibid., 520.
50. Ibid., 521.
51. Ibid., 125. As is indicated in Hildreth's *The Slave*, the theme of infanticide under the pressures of slavery was already commonplace in abolitionist literature, inspired as it was from news accounts of such acts of desperation. William Wells Brown offers one early example in his *Narrative* of a slave woman who was separated from her husband

and children and shipped aboard a slaver to New Orleans. Brown writes that "having no desire to live without them, in the agony of her soul [she] jumped overboard and drowned herself" (20). Of course, the most recent instance of the theme in American literature is Toni Morrison's retelling in *Beloved* of the story of Margaret Garner, an Ohio slave who murdered one of her children in 1856. See Angelita Reyes, "Using History as Artifact to Situate Beloved's Unknown Women," 77–85; Cynthia Griffin Wolff, "'Margaret Garner,'" 105–122.

52. Stowe, *Uncle Tom's Cabin*, 560.
53. Ibid., 45.
54. Ibid., 57.
55. Thus, on the level of their adherence to the ideological imperatives of domestic ideology, Eliza and Cassy (at least until Cassy's Christian conversion) are, to a certain degree, held up as foils in a manner parallel to that in which Tom and George are frequently contrasted with respect to their degree of political agency. For a discussion of the male protagonists' bifurcation in *Uncle Tom's Cabin*, see Stepto, "Sharing the Thunder," 136; Yarborough, "Strategies of Black Characterization," 53.
56. Mullen, "Runaway Tongue," 244–264, 255.
57. Stowe, *Uncle Tom's Cabin*, 502, 504, 506.
58. In this section of the novel, Cassy demonstrates a degree of autonomy and agency more like Stowe's mixed-race masculine hero, George Harris. Ultimately, for Stowe, Cassy represents a departure from the gender stereotype of the "tragic mulatta" more than the racial stereotype of the mixed-race subject more broadly. Thanks to Michael Bennett for this observation.
59. Wardley continues: "Stowe's belief that some spirit inhabits all things is not only an exoticized import from the Roman Catholic and African American religions of New Orleans and beyond. It is by 1852 one familiar element of the nineteenth century domestic ideology the tenets of which Stowe's writing reflected and helped to shape." See Lynn Wardley, "Relic Fetish, Femmage," 203–220.
60. Stowe, *Uncle Tom's Cabin*, 504, 506, 511, 512.
61. Ibid., 525.
62. Ibid., 527.
63. Initially, Cassy tries to persuade Tom to do away with Legree using the ax she has strategically placed by the back door. Tom refuses, horrified by the prospect of violating his principles of Christian brotherhood. He nonetheless sanctions Cassy's escape attempt, so long as she can accomplish it without "blood-guiltiness." In this way, Stowe seems to confer her blessing, through Tom, upon Cassy's less violent, yet equally powerful, form of rebellion.
64. Stowe, *Uncle Tom's Cabin*, 566, 567. For a discussion of the cultural implications of the gendered "madwoman" plot in *Uncle Tom's*

Cabin, see Sandra M. Gilbert and Susan Gubar, *The Madwoman in the Attic.* Gilbert and Gubar argue that Cassy "exploits impersonation of madness and confinement to escape maddening confinement" (534).

65. Stowe, *Uncle Tom's Cabin,* 567–568.
66. Ibid., 595.
67. Ibid., 597.
68. Wardley, "Relic Fetish, Femmage," 214.
69. Like many of his contemporaries, Beecher considered himself both an abolitionist and a colonizationist. See Hedrick, *Harriet Beecher Stowe,* 103–104. It is, of course, a mistake to minimize the liberatory function to Stowe of evangelical Protestantism. Among other purposes, it serves as a corrective in *Uncle Tom's Cabin* to the kind of rampant moral contagion represented by Legree. For a useful discussion of Stowe's evolving theological beliefs and their relation to her writing, see Carolyn Haynes, "The Inclusive Community." See also Patricia R. Hill, "Lightning on a Landscape."
70. Stowe, *Uncle Tom's Cabin,* 607.
71. Ibid., 608.
72. Brown, *Domestic Individualism,* 59.
73. I am indebted to Andrea K. Newlyn for this insight. See "Becoming An/Other."
74. Hildreth, *The Slave,* 2:159.
75. Ibid., 2:162.
76. In 1852, a Boston publishing house that had formerly rejected *The Slave* tried to capitalize on the runaway success of *Uncle Tom's Cabin* by issuing a new edition of Hildreth's work, complete with a sequel in which Archy returns to America to search for Cassy and their son, Montgomery. If anything, the sequel is even more incendiary than the original narrative. It includes a scene in which Thomas, still on the run, is burned alive by an angry mob. In contradistinction to Stowe's work, it argues explicitly against colonization and for immediate emancipation as a prerequisite for the continuance of American democracy. In the end, the family is successfully reunited and includes a character named Eliza, who is engaged to be married to the young Montgomery. For a comparison of the sequel to the original, see Yellin, *The Intricate Knot,* 109–116.

CHAPTER 4 PUBLIC POOR RELIEF AND NATIONAL BELONGING IN HARRIET WILSON'S *OUR NIG*

1. Eric Foner, *Politics and Ideology in the Age of the Civil War,* 67. On the relationship between slavery, the antebellum labor movement, and the white working class, see also David R. Roediger, *The Wages of Whiteness,* 66–100.
2. Foner, *Politics and Ideology,* 60.

3. On the story of Gates's discovery of *Our Nig* in a Manhattan book-shop in 1981, see Henry Louis Gates Jr., *Figures in Black*, 125–126.
4. Wilson, *Our Nig*, n.p.
5. Gates, *Figures in Black*, 147.
6. Wilson, *Our Nig*, 134.
7. Gates, *Figures in Black*, 146.
8. Wilson, *Our Nig*, 122, 105, 109.
9. Though "outdoor relief" often meant the removal of the pauper to another dwelling, it was also possible for the town to subsidize the recipient to allow him or her to stay at home. See Timothy Dodge, "Poor Relief in Durham, Lee, and Madbury."
10. Such contracts, rather than "ensuring fair play" or "benefiting the child," usually stipulated minimum standards, such as length of servitude and schooling minimums. See Dodge, "Poor Relief in Durham," 8. See also Marcus Wilson Jernegan, *Laboring and Dependent Classes in Colonial America*, 106–112.
11. George Plummer Hadley, *The History of the Town of Goffstown*, 183. In her excellent study of the abolitionist Hayward family that probably served as a model for the Bellmonts, Barbara A. White confirms that according to both external and internal evidence, Frado was indeed "bound out" to the Bellmonts ("'Our Nig' and the She-Devil," n.9). White must also be credited for her insight that "economic motives predominate" in the novel. See White, "'Our Nig' and the She-Devil."
12. Though Gates cites Wilson's association with the Goffstown poorhouse, he oddly refers to the Bellmonts as Frado's "foster family" (Wilson, *Our Nig*, xix).
13. For representative studies, see Claudia Tate, "Allegories of Black Female Desire"; Carby, *Reconstructing Womanhood*; Beth Maclay Doriani, "Black Womanhood in Nineteenth-Century America"; Frances Smith Foster, *Written By Herself*. Gates notes that "the great evil in this book is not love-betrayed, however, or the evils of the flesh; rather, it is poverty, both the desperation it inflicts as well as the evils it implicitly sanctions, which is *Our Nig*'s focus of social commentary" (Wilson, *Our Nig*, xlvi).
14. George Ramsdell, *The History of Milford*, 74–75.
15. Hadley, *The History of the Town of Goffstown*, 185–186.
16. James H. Oliver, *Free People of Color*, 124. On the intensifying race antagonism between free blacks and working-class Northern whites, see Roediger, *The Wages of Whiteness*, 57–60. On how free blacks lost out to Irish Americans in the competition for jobs, see Roediger, *The Wages of Whiteness*, 147–148. On how antebellum blackface minstrelsy assuaged an acute sense of class insecurity by indulging feelings of racial superiority, see Eric Lott, *Love and Theft*, 64.
17. Qtd. in Dodge, "Poor Relief in Durham," 35–36.

18. Wilson, *Our Nig*, 1, 6.
19. See Cathy N. Davidson, *Revolution and the Word*, 125–126.
20. Wilson, *Our Nig*, 7, 9.
21. Dodge, "Poor Relief in Durham," 12–13; emphasis mine. In addition to poor relief, charitable societies were established during this period to help people with alcoholism, those considered insane, free blacks and slaves, orphans, immigrants, and others. See also Joseph Benjamin Klebaner, *Public Poor Relief in America*.
22. Wilson, *Our Nig*, 8.
23. Dodge, "Poor Relief in Durham," 13.
24. Hadley, *The History of the Town of Goffstown*, 185–186. The Goffstown farm continued to serve as the county poorhouse until it was sold at auction in 1866. Hadley vacillates concerning his views of the treatment accorded occupants of the poorhouse. At one time, he waxes lyrical about "those dependent upon public charity and the unfortunate" and quotes Cicero's orations: "O Tempora, O mores." At another point, he determines that "the inmates received all they could naturally expect" (187).
25. Wilson, *Our Nig*, 8.
26. Qtd. in Gates, *Figures in Black*, 142. To Gates, it "seems curious that Mag Smith's condition assumes a precedent over Frado's, until we recall that the action of the plot is set in motion by Mag's unmarried pregnancy" (143).
27. Gates, *Figures in Black*, xxviii. Likewise, in *Amalgamation!* James Kinney remarks that Wilson "introduces the motif of the willing sexual relationship between a white woman and a black man" (100). At times, critics appear bemused as to the import of the biracial configuration represented by Mag and Jim. Illustratively, Frances Smith Foster notes cursorily in *Written by Herself* that "this was an important difference in the literary depiction of the mulatto and it was an unusual coda to the plot of the sentimental novel" (87). Yet such claims to the novel's singularity in this regard overlook the tradition of interracial fiction that Lydia Maria Child inaugurated with *Hobomok* in 1824 and later popularized in stories and novels featuring mixed-race characters. See chapter 1.
28. Foster, *Written by Herself*, 88.
29. Wilson, *Our Nig*, 12.
30. Ibid., 13.
31. Ibid., 16–17.
32. Ibid., 28.
33. For example, Claudia Tate contends that Frado's "psychic liberation occurs when she refuses to accept passively Mrs. Bellmont's repeated abuse." However, she qualifies the import of Frado's act of "self-affirmation," which she views as "fundamentally compromised" in that it fails to reflect women's "collective fantasies about their history and reality." See "Allegories of Black Female Desire," 105. Re-

ferring to the same scene, Beth Maclay Doriani argues that "although Mrs. Bellmont continues physically and emotionally to abuse her, Frado shows that her spirit cannot be broken" ("Black Womanhood," 216).

34. Qtd. in Jernegan, *Laboring and Dependent Classes*, 112.
35. Jernegan, *Laboring and Dependent Classes*, 128. Though such statutes favored male over female education, they nonetheless specify at least a modicum of literacy education for both sexes.
36. Wilson, *Our Nig*, 31–32.
37. Ibid., 31.
38. Ibid., 31, 32.
39. Ibid., 32.
40. Ibid., 33.
41. Ibid.
42. Ibid.
43. Ibid., 38.
44. Ibid., 88.
45. Lawrence A. Cremin, *American Education*, 138, 351.
46. Here I am thinking of the work of such critics as Jean Fagan Yellin and Carolyn L. Karcher, who argue that the "tragic mulatto" figure carries the added burden of exemplifying nineteenth-century standards of white bourgeois femininity. See Yellin, *Women and Sisters*; Karcher, "Lydia Maria Child's *Romance of the Republic*." For the originary discussion of the term, see Barbara Welter, "The Cult of True Womanhood," 151–174.
47. Cynthia J. Davis, "Speaking the Body's Pain," 391–404.
48. John Ernest argues rightly that scenes such as this serve to unmask "tyrannical employers," thus returning "economic relations to their moral grounds" ("Economies of Identity," 435).
49. Wilson, *Our Nig*, 72.
50. Ibid., 85.
51. Ibid., 74.
52. Ibid., 95.
53. Ibid., 116, 119, 120.
54. Ibid., 129, 130, 137.
55. Ibid., 130.
56. Ibid., 109.
57. Cremin, *American Education*, 94.
58. Wilson, *Our Nig*, 137, 140.
59. For example, Gates argues that Wilson allows the racist Bellmonts to name the protagonist, "only to invert such racism by employing the name, in inverted commas, as her pseudonym of authorship" (Wilson, *Our Nig*, li).
60. Hazel Carby, for instance, sees *Our Nig* as an "allegory of a slave narrative," where the Bellmont house "increasingly resembles the nation, as the resolve of Mrs. Bellmont's opponents to improve Frado's

conditions disintegrated at the slightest possibility of conflict." Thus, to Carby, the allegory is intended to reveal the failure of Northern abolitionism rather than to point toward any ameliorating, emancipatory social alternative. See *Reconstructing Womanhood*, 44. On *Our Nig* as satire, see Elizabeth Breau, "Identifying Satire," 455–466. Breau makes the essential point that "the expectation that nineteenth-century black-authored first-person narratives contain only unaltered truth restricts our ability to see the authors of such texts as creative artists and confines them to the limiting role of political advocates who did their inadequate best with the existing white literary tradition" (458).

CODA: THE "TRAGIC MULATTA" THEN AND NOW

1. James Dao, "A Family Get-Together of Historic Proportions," *New York Times*, July 14, 2003.
2. Herbert Gutman is one such historian, who writes that Southern court records containing divorce suits that include an accounting of slaves suggest that lasting relationships between masters and slaves "were not rare." See *The Black Family in Slavery and Freedom*, 419.
3. The scandal began with the exposure of the liaison in 1802 in the *Richmond (Virginia) Recorder* by Federalist sympathizer John Thomson Callender. See Brodie, *Thomas Jefferson*, 348–349.
4. See Andrews, *Sally Hemings*, 98; *Sally Hemings: An American Scandal*; *Jefferson in Paris*.
5. This amorous depiction accords with that of Fawn M. Brodie, who writes that Hemings "was certainly lonely in Paris, as well as supremely ready for the first great love of her life, and she was living daily in the presence of a man who was by nature tender and gallant with all women. For any slave child at Monticello Jefferson was a kind of deity" (*Thomas Jefferson*, 228).
6. Far from the romantic renderings of the union prevalent in mass-media productions, Steve Erickson's novel *Arc d'X* enacts a violent rape of Hemings at Jefferson's hands. Afterward, the narrator speaks for the statesman in musing that "it was the nature of American freedom that he was only free to take his pleasure in something he possessed, in the same way it would ultimately be the nature of America to define itself in terms of what was owned" (38).
7. Brodie, *Thomas Jefferson*, 82–83.
8. Jefferson vows to emancipate James if he returns to Virginia with Sally once he learns the art of French cuisine, though, in reality, seven years passed before Jefferson freed him. There is no record that Jefferson ever freed Sally. On the contrary, she is not mentioned in Jefferson's will. Instead, after his death she appears on the official slave inventory of 1827 as worth $50. It is his daughter, Martha, who finally arranges Sally's emancipation two years after her father's de-

mise. At the time, freeing a slave without special permission from the legislature meant automatic banishment from Virginia for an abolitionist sympathizer. Brodie speculates that Jefferson delayed such a move to avoid the certain publicity that would follow about his already infamous relations with a slave (*Thomas Jefferson*, 235, 466–467).

9. Tina Andrews played the part of Valerie Grant on *Days of Our Lives* beginning in 1983. After the character kissed the son of the lead white female character on the show, NBC executives issued an order that "there should be no evidence of open mouth kissing." By the next year, after a rash of hate mail, the story line was changed, and Andrews's part was eliminated. See Tina Andrews, *Sally Hemings*, 12–13.

10. Andrews, *Sally Hemings*, 78.

11. Ibid., 33.

12. *Black Issues in Higher Education*, 19. See also David Mehegan, "Wind Chill," *Boston Globe*, April 18, 2000; Jeffrey D. Grosset, "*The Wind Done Gone*," 1113–1131.

13. Grosset, "*The Wind Done Gone*," 1125.

14. Randall, *The Wind Done Gone*, 128.

15. Alice Randall, interview by Terri Gross, *Fresh Air*, National Public Radio, July 14, 2001.

16. Randall, *The Wind Done Gone*, 16, 47.

17. Ibid., 48.

18. Ibid., 162.

19. Ibid., 109–110.

BIBLIOGRAPHY

Anderson, Margo J. *The American Census: A Social History*. New Haven, Conn.: Yale University Press, 1988.

Anderson, Margo J., and Stephen E. Fienberg, eds. *Who Counts?: The Politics of Census-Taking in Contemporary America*. New York: Russell Sage Foundation, 1999.

Andrews, Tina. *Sally Hemings: An American Scandal: The Struggle to Tell the Controversial True Story*. New York: Malibu Press, 2001.

Andrews, William, L. "Inter(racial)textuality in Nineteenth-Century Southern Narrative." In *Influence and Intertextuality in Literary History*, edited by Jay Clayton and Eric Rothstein, 298–317. Madison: University of Wisconsin Press, 1991.

———. "The Novelization of Voice in Early African Narrative." *PMLA* 105 (1990): 23–34.

Balibar, Etienne, and Immanel Wallerstein. *Race, Nation, Class: Ambiguous Identities*. London: Verso, 1991.

Baym, Nina. *Woman's Fiction: A Guide to Novels by and about Women in America, 1820–1870*. Ithaca, N.Y.: Cornell University Press, 1978.

Beam, Dorri Rabung. "The Flower of Black Female Sexuality in Pauline Hopkins's *Winona*." In *Recovering the Black Female Body: Self-Representations by African American Women,* edited by Michael Bennett and Vanessa D. Dickerson, 71–96. New Brunswick, N.J.: Rutgers University Press, 2001.

Bennett, Michael, and Vanessa D. Dickerson, eds. *Recovering the Black Female Body: Self-Representations by African American Women*. New Brunswick, N.J.: Rutgers University Press, 2001.

Berlant, Lauren. "Poor Eliza." *American Literature* 70.3: 635–668.

Berzon, Judith R. *Neither White Nor Black: The Mulatto Character in American Fiction*. New York: New York University Press, 1978.

Black Issues in Higher Education 19.8 (June 6, 2002): 19.

Breau, Elizabeth. "Identifying Satire: Our Nig." *Callaloo* 16.2 (1993): 455–466.

Brodie, Fawn M. *Thomas Jefferson: An Intimate History*. New York: Norton, 1974.

Brody, Jennifer DeVere. *Impossible Purities: Blackness, Femininity, and Victorian Culture.* Durham, N.C.: Duke University Press, 1998.

Brown, Gillian. *Domestic Individualism: Imagining Self in Nineteenth-Century America.* Berkeley and Los Angeles: University of California Press, 1990.

Brown, Sterling. *The Negro in American Fiction.* Washington, D.C.: Associates in Negro Folk Education, 1937.

———. *Negro Poetry and Drama.* 1937; reprinted in *The Negro in American Poetry.* New York: Atheneum, 1969.

Brown, William Wells. *Clotel; or, The President's Daughter, A Narrative of Slave Life in the United States.* New York: University Books, 1969.

———. *Narrative of the Life and Escape of William Wells Brown* in *Clotel; or, The President's Daughter, A Narrative of Slave Life in the United States.* New York: University Books, 1969.

Burg, B. R. "The Rhetoric of Miscegenation: Thomas Jefferson, Sally Hemings, and Their Historians." *Phylon* 47.2 (1986): 128–138.

Carby, Hazel V. *Reconstructing Womanhood: The Emergence of the Afro-American Woman Novelist.* New York: Oxford University Press, 1987.

Castiglia, Christopher. *Bound and Determined.* Chicago: University of Chicago Press, 1996.

Child, Lydia Maria. *An Appeal in Favor of That Class of Americans Called Africans.* Edited by Carolyn L. Karcher. Amherst: University of Massachusetts Press, 1996.

———. *Hobomok and Other Writings on Indians.* Edited by Carolyn L. Karcher. New York: Rutgers University Press, 1986.

———. "The Quadroons." *Liberty Bell.* Boston: Boston Anti-Slavery Society, 1842; reprinted in *Fact and Fiction.* New York: C. S. Francis, 1846.

———. *A Romance of the Republic.* Boston: Ticknor and Fields, 1867. Reprint, Miami: Mnemosyne Press, 1969.

———. *Selected Letters, 1817–1880.* Edited by Milton Meltzer and Patricia G. Holland. Amherst: University of Massachusetts Press, 1982.

———. "Slavery's Pleasant Homes." *Liberty Bell.* Boston: Massachusetts Anti-Slavery Fair, 1843.

———. "Willie Wharton." *Atlantic Monthly,* March 1863, 324–345.

Chinn, Sarah. *Technology and the Logic of American Racism: A Cultural History of the Body as Evidence.* London: Continuum, 2000.

Christian, Barbara. *Black Women Novelists: The Development of a Tradition, 1892–1976.* Westport, Conn.: Greenwood, 1980.

Clifford, Deborah Pickman. *Crusader for Freedom: A Life of Lydia Maria Child.* Boston: Beacon Press, 1992.

Crafts, Hannah. *The Bondwoman's Narrative.* New York: Warner Books, 2002.

Cremin, Lawrence A. *American Education: The National Experience, 1783–1876.* New York: Harper and Row, 1980.

Crenshaw, Kimberle, Neil Gotenda, Gary Peller, and Kendall Thomas, eds. *Critical Race Theory: The Key Writings That Formed the Movement.* New York: Free Press, 1995.

Cvetkovich, Ann. *Mixed Feelings: Feminism, Mass Culture, and Victorian Sensationalism.* New Brunswick, N.J.: Rutgers University Press, 1992.

Dao, James. "A Family Get-Together of Historic Proportions: Monticello Greets Kin of Jefferson's Slave." *New York Times,* July 14, 2003.

Davidson, Cathy N. *Revolution and the Word: The Rise of the Novel in America.* New York: Oxford University Press, 1986.

Davis, Cynthia J. "Speaking the Body's Pain": Harriet Wilson's *Our Nig.*" *African American Review* 27.3 (1993): 391–404.

Davis, James F. *Who Is Black: One Nation's Definition.* University Park: Pennsylvania State University Press, 1991.

Dimock, Wai-Chee. "Feminism, New Historicism, and the Reader." *American Literature* 63.4 (1991): 601–622.

Dodge, Timothy. "Poor Relief in Durham, Lee, and Madbury, 1732–1891." Master's thesis, University of New Hampshire, 1982.

Doriani, Beth Maclay. "Black Womanhood in Nineteenth-Century America: Subversion and Self-Construction in Two Women's Autobiographies." *American Quarterly* 43.2 (1991): 199–222.

duCille, Ann. *The Coupling Convention: Sex, Text, and Tradition in Black Women's Fiction.* New York: Oxford University Press, 1993.

———. "Where in the World Is William Wells Brown? Thomas Jefferson, Sally Hemings, and the DNA of African-American Literary History." *American Literary History* 12.3 (Fall 2000): 443–462.

Duffy, Brian. "Jefferson's Secret Life." *U.S. News & World Report,* November 9, 1998, 58.

Elder, Arlene A. *"Hindered Hand": Cultural Implications of Early African American Fiction.* Westport, Conn.: Greenwood Press, 1978.

Erickson, Steve. *Arc D'X.* New York: Poseidon Press, 1993.

Ernest, John. "Economies of Identity: Harriet Wilson's *Our Nig.*" *PMLA* 109.3 (1994): 424–438.

Felski, Rita. *The Gender of Modernity.* Cambridge, Mass.: Harvard University Press, 1995.

Farrison, William. *William Wells Brown: Author and Reformer.* Chicago: University of Chicago Press, 1969.

Foner, Eric. *Free Soil, Free Labor, Free Men: The Ideology of the Republican Party before the Civil War.* New York: Oxford University Press, 1970.

———. *Politics and Ideology in the Age of the Civil War.* New York: Oxford University Press, 1980.

Bibliography

————. *Reconstruction: America's Unfinished Revolution, 1863–1877*. New York: Harper and Row, 1988.

Foster, Frances Smith. *Written By Herself: Literary Production by African American Women, 1746–1892*. Bloomington: Indiana University Press, 1993.

Fredrickson, George M. *The Black Image in the White Mind: The Debate on Afro-American Character and Destiny, 1817–1914*. Middleton, Conn.: Wesleyan University Press, 1971.

————. *White Supremacy: A Comparative Study of American and South African History*. New York: Oxford University Press, 1981.

Funderburg, Lise. *Black, White, Other: Biracial Americans Talk About Race and Identity*. New York: William Morrow, 1994.

Garber, Marjorie. *Vested Interests: Cross-Dressing and Cultural Anxiety*. New York: Routledge, 1992.

Gates, Henry Louis, Jr. *Figures in Black: Words, Signs, and the "Racial" Self*. New York: Oxford University Press, 1987.

Gerber, David A. *Black Ohio and the Color Line, 1860–1915*. Urbana: University of Illinois Press, 1976.

Gilbert, Sandra M., and Susan Gubar. *The Madwoman in the Attic: The Woman Writer and the Nineteenth-Century Literary Imagination*. New Haven, Conn.: Yale University Press, 1979.

Gilman, Susan. "The Mulatto, Tragic or Triumphant? The Nineteenth-Century Race Melodrama." In *The Culture of Sentiment: Race, Gender, and Sentimentality in Nineteenth-Century America*, edited by Shirley Samuels, 221–243. New York: Oxford University Press, 1992.

Gordon-Reed, Annette. "Engaging Jefferson: Blacks and the Founding Father." *William and Mary Quarterly*, 3rd ser., 57.1 (2000): 171–182.

Grant, Mary. *North Over South: Northern Nationalism and American Identity in the Antebellum Era*. Lawrence: University Press of Kansas, 2000.

Grosset, Jeffrey D. "*The Wind Done Gone*: Transforming Tara into Plantation Parody." *Case Western Law Review* 52.4 (Summer 2002): 1113–1131.

Gutman, Herbert. *The Black Family in Slavery and Freedom, 1750–1925*. New York: Vintage Books, 1976.

Hadley, George Plummer. *The History of the Town of Goffstown, 1733–1920*. Concord, Mass.: Rumford, 1922.

Haizlip, Shirlee Taylor. *The Sweeter the Juice: A Family Memoir in Black and White*. New York: Touchstone Books, 1995.

Haynes, Carolyn. "The Inclusive Community: Harriet Beecher Stowe's Redefinition of Christianity and Woman in *The Minister's Wooing*." Ph.D. diss., University of California, San Diego, 1990.

Hedrick, Joan. *Harriet Beecher Stowe: A Life*. New York: Oxford University Press, 1994.

Higginbotham, A. Leon, Jr., and Barbara K. Kopytoff. "Racial Purity and Interracial Sex in the Law in Colonial and Antebellum Virginia." In *Interracialism: Black-White Intermarriage in American History, Literature and Law*, edited by Werner Sollors, 81–139. Oxford: Oxford University Press, 2000.

Hildreth, Richard. *Despotism in America: An Inquiry into the Nature, Results, and Legal Basis of the Slave-Holding System in the United States*. Boston: J. P. Jewett, 1854.

———. *The Slave; or, Memoirs of Archy Moore*. 2 vols. Boston: John H. Eastburn, 1836. Upper Saddle River, N.J.: Upper Saddle River Press, 1968.

———. *The White Slave; or, Memoirs of a Fugitive*. New York: Miller, Orton & Mulligan, 1855.

Hill, Patricia R. "Lightning on a Landscape: Revisioning the World of Harriet Beecher Stowe." Unpublished manuscript, in the author's possession.

Holt, Michael F. *The Political Crisis of the 1850s*. New York: John Wiley, 1978.

Horsman, Reginald. *Race and Manifest Destiny: The Origins of American Racial Anglo-Saxonism*. Cambridge, Mass.: Harvard University Press, 1981.

Jefferson in Paris. Directed by James Ivory. Hollywood, Calif.: Touchstone Pictures, 1995.

Jernegan, Marcus Wilson. *Laboring and Dependent Classes in Colonial America*. New York: Frederick Unger, 1931; second printing, 1965.

Jones, Lisa. "Are We Tiger Woods Yet?" *Village Voice*, July 7, 1997, 36.

Jones, Vanessa E. "A Rich Sense of Self: Many in New Generation of Biracial People Reject Narrow Categorizations." *Boston Globe*, February 29, 2000.

Jordan, Winthrop D. *White Over Black: American Attitudes toward the Negro, 1550–1812*. Chapel Hill: University of North Carolina Press, 1968.

Kaplan, Amy. "Manifest Domesticity." *American Literature* 70.3 (September 1998): 581–606.

Kaplan, Sidney. "The Miscegenation Issue in the Election of 1864." In *American Studies in Black and White*, edited by Allan D. Austin, 47–100. Amherst: University of Massachusetts Press, 1991.

Karcher, Carolyn L. *The First Woman of the Republic: A Cultural Biography of Lydia Maria Child*. Durham, N.C.: Duke University Press, 1994.

———. "Lydia Maria Child's *Romance of the Republic*: An Abolitionist Vision of America's Racial Destiny." In *Slavery and the Literary Imagination*, edited by Deborah E. McDowell and Arnold Rampersad, 88–103. Baltimore: Johns Hopkins University Press, 1987.

———. "Rape, Murder, Revenge in 'Slavery's Pleasant Homes': Lydia

Maria Child's Antislavery Fiction and the Limits of Genre." *Women's Studies International Forum* 9.4 (1986): 323–332.

———, ed. *Hobomok and Other Writings on Indians*. New Brunswick, N.J.: Rutgers University Press, 1986.

———. *A Lydia Maria Child Reader*. Durham, N.C.: Duke University Press, 1997.

Kellow, Margaret R. "Duties Are Ours: A Life of Lydia Maria Child." Ph.D. diss., Yale University, 1994.

Kinney, James. *Amalgamation! Race, Sex and Rhetoric in the Nineteenth-Century American Novel*. Westport, Conn.: Greenwood Press, 1985.

Kirkham, Bruce. *The Building of Uncle Tom's Cabin*. Knoxville: University of Tennessee Press, 1977.

Klebaner, Joseph Benjamin. *Public Poor Relief in America, 1790–1860*. New York: Arno Press, 1976.

Lemire, Ellen. *"Miscegenation": Making Race in America*. Philadelphia: University of Pennsylvania Press, 2002.

Litwack, Leon F. *North of Slavery: The Negro in the Free States, 1790–1860*. Chicago: University of Chicago Press, 1961.

Loggins, Vernon. *The Negro Author: His Development in America*. New York: Columbia University Press, 1931.

Lohmann, Christoph K. *Discovering Difference: Contemporary Essays in American Culture*. Bloomington: Indiana University Press, 1993.

Lopez, Ian Haney. *White by Law: The Legal Construction of Race*. New York: New York University Press, 1996.

Lott, Eric. *Love and Theft: Blackface Minstrelsy and the American Working Class*. New York: Oxford University Press, 1993.

Malcolmson, Scott L. *One Drop of Blood: The Misadventure of Race*. New York: Farrar, Strauss, Giroux, 2000.

McBride, James. *The Color of Water: A Black Man's Tribute to His White Mother*. New York: Riverhead Books, 1996.

McKay, Nellie Y., and Kathryn Earle. *Approaches to Teaching the Novels of Toni Morrison*. New York: Modern Language Association of America, 1997.

Mehegan, David. "Wind Chill." *Boston Globe*, April 18, 2000.

Mills, Bruce. *Cultural Reformations: Lydia Maria Child and the Literature of Reform*. Athens: University of Georgia Press, 1994.

———. "Lydia Maria Child and the Endings to Harriet Jacobs' *Incidents in the Life of a Slave Girl*." *American Literature* 64.2 (1992): 255–271.

Moran, Rachel F. *Interracial Intimacy: The Regulation of Race and Romance*. Chicago: University of Chicago Press, 2001.

Morison, Samuel Eliot, and Henry Steel Commager. *The Growth of the American Republic*. Vol. 1. New York: Oxford University Press, 1930.

Nelson, Dana. *The Word in Black and White: Reading "Race" in American Literature, 1638–1867.* New York: Oxford University Press, 1992.

Newlyn, Andrea K. "Becoming An/Other: Theories of Transracial Embodiment and Narrative Form." Unpublished manuscript, in the author's possession.

Nobles, Melissa. *Shades of Citizenship.* Stanford, Calif.: Stanford University Press, 2000.

O'Connell, Catherine E. "'The Magic of the Real Presence of Distress': Sentimentality and Competing Rhetorics of Authority." In *The Stowe Debate*, edited by Mason I. Lowance Jr. and Ellen E. Westbrook, 13–36. Amherst: University of Massachusetts Press, 1994.

Oliver, James H. *Free People of Color: Inside the African American Community.* Washington, D.C.: Smithsonian Institution Press, 1993.

Peterson, Carla L. *"Doers of the Word": African American Women Speakers and Writers in the North (1830–1880).* New York: Oxford University Press, 1995.

Quarles, Benjamin. *Black Abolitionists.* New York: Oxford University Press, 1969.

Raimon, Eve. "*Miscegenation*, 'Melaleukation' and Public Reception." In *Fear Itself: Enemies Real and Imagined in American Culture*, edited by Nancy Lusignan Schultz, 121–132. West Lafayette, Ind.: Purdue University Press, 1999.

Ramsdell, George. *The History of Milford.* Concord, Mass.: Rumford, 1901.

Randall, Alice. *The Wind Done Gone.* Boston: Houghton Mifflin, 2001.

"Redefining Race in America." *Newsweek*, September 18, 2000, 38–65.

Reyes, Angelita. "Using History as Artifact to Situate *Beloved*'s Unknown Women." In *Approaches to Teaching the Novels of Toni Morrison*, edited by Nellie Y. McKay and Kathryn Earle, 77–85. New York: Modern Language Association of America, 1997.

Robertson, Tatsha. "Minorities Fear Census Falls Short." *Boston Globe*, June 30, 1999.

Rodriguez, Cindy. "Civil Rights Groups Wary of Census Data on Race." *Boston Globe*, December 8, 2000.

Roediger, David R. *The Wages of Whiteness: Race and the Making of the American Working Class.* London: Verso, 1991.

Rose, Ann C. *Transcendentalism as a Social Movement, 1830–1850.* New Haven, Conn.: Yale University Press, 1981.

Saks, Eva. "Representing Miscegenation Law." *Raritan* 8.2 (1988): 39–69.

Sale, Maggie. "Critiques from Within: Antebellum Projects of Resistance." *American Literature* 64.4 (1992): 696–718.

Sally Hemings: An American Scandal. Directed by Charles Haid. Hollywood, Calif.: Artisan Productions, 2000.

Samuels, Shirley, ed., *The Culture of Sentiment: Race, Gender, and Sentimentality in Nineteenth-Century America*. New York: Oxford University Press, 1992.

Sánchez-Eppler, Karen. "Bodily Bonds: The Intersecting Rhetorics of Feminism and Abolition." *Representations* 24 (1988): 28–59.

—————. *Touching Liberty: Abolition, Feminism, and the Politics of the Body*. Berkeley and Los Angeles: University of California Press, 1993.

Sejour, Victor. "Le Mulatre, 1837." *Revue de Louisiane* 1.2 (Winter 1972): 60–75.

Senna, Danzy. *Caucasia*. New York: Riverhead Books, 1998.

Sewell, Richard H. *Ballots for Freedom: Antislavery Politics in the United States, 1837–1860*. New York: Oxford University Press, 1976.

Sollors, Werner. *Neither Black Nor White Yet Both: Thematic Explorations of Interracial Literature*. New York: Oxford University Press, 1997.

—————, ed. *Interracialism: Black-White Intermarriage in American History, Literature and Law*. Oxford: Oxford University Press, 2000.

Smith, Barbara Hernnstein. *On the Margins of Discourse*. Chicago: University of Chicago Press, 1978.

Stedman, John Gabriel. *Narrative of Joanna, An Emancipated Slave of Surinam*. Boston: Isaac Knapp, 1838.

Stephanson, Anders. *Manifest Destiny: American Expansion and the Empire of Right*. New York: Hill and Wang, 1995.

Stepto, Robert B. "Sharing the Thunder: The Literary Exchanges of Harriet Beecher Stowe, Henry Bibb, and Frederick Douglass." In *New Essays on* Uncle Tom's Cabin, edited by Eric. J. Sundquist, 135–153. Cambridge: Cambridge University Press, 1986.

Stokes, Mason. *The Color of Sex: Whiteness, Heterosexuality, and the Fictions of White Supremacy*. Durham, N.C.: Duke University Press, 2001.

Stowe, Harriet Beecher. *The Key to Uncle Tom's Cabin*. Boston: J. P. Jewett, 1853.

—————. *Uncle Tom's Cabin; or, Life Among the Lowly*. 1852. Reprint, New York: Penguin, 1981.

Sundquist, Eric J., ed. *New Essays on* Uncle Tom's Cabin. Cambridge: Cambridge University Press, 1986.

Takaki, Ronald, T. *Iron Cages: Race and Culture in Nineteenth-Century America*. New York: Alfred A. Knopf, 1979.

Tate, Claudia. "Allegories of Black Female Desire." In *Changing Our Own Words: Essays on Criticism, Theory, and Writing by Black Women*, 98–126. New Brunswick, N.J.: Rutgers University Press, 1989.

Tompkins, Jane. *Sensational Designs: The Cultural Work of American Fiction, 1790–1860*. New York: Oxford University Press, 1985.

Wall, Cheryl, ed. *Changing Our Own Words: Essays on Criticism Theory, and*

Writing by Black Women. New Brunswick, N.J.: Rutgers University Press, 1989.

Wardley, Lynn. "Relic Fetish, Femmage: The Aesthetics of Sentiment in the Work of Stowe." In *The Culture of Sentiment*, edited by Shirley Samuels, 203–220. New York: Oxford University Press, 1992.

Welter, Barbara. "The Cult of True Womanhood: 1820–1860." *Atlantic Monthly* 18.2 (Summer 1966): 151–174.

Werner, John M. *Reaping the Bloody Harvest: Race Riots in the United States during the Age of Jackson, 1824–1849*. New York: Garland, 1986.

White, Barbara A. "'Our Nig' and the She-Devil: New Information about Harriet Wilson and the Bellmont Family." *American Literature* 65.1 (1993): 19–52.

Williamson, Joel. *New People: Miscegenation and Mulattos in the United States*. New York: New York University Press, 1984.

Wilson, Harriet. *Our Nig; or, Sketches from the Life of a Free Black in a Two-Story White House, North, Showing That Slavery's Shadows Fall Even There*. Boston: George C. Rand and Avery, 1859. Reprint, New York: Vintage Books, 1983.

Wolff, Cynthia Griffin. "'Margaret Garner': A Cincinnati Story." In *Discovering Difference: Contemporary Essays in American Culture*, edited by Christoph K. Lohmann, 105–132. Bloomington: Indiana University Press, 1993.

Yarborough, Richard. "Strategies of Black Characterization." In *New Essays on Uncle Tom's Cabin*, edited by Eric J. Sundquist, 45–84. Cambridge: Cambridge University Press, 1986.

Yellin, Jean Fagan. *The Intricate Knot: Black Figures in American Literature*. New York: New York University Press, 1972.

———. *Women and Sisters: The Antislavery Feminists in American Culture*. New Haven, Conn.: Yale University Press, 1989.

Zackodnik, Teresa. "Fixing the Color Line: The Mulatto, Southern Courts, and Racial Identity." *American Quarterly* 53.3 (2001): 420–451.

Zanger, Jules. "The Tragic Octoroon in Pre–Civil War Fiction." *American Quarterly* 18.1 (Spring 1966): 63–70.

Index

abolitionism/abolitionist writing:
in Brown, 70, 77, 82, 85, 86; in
Child, 14, 18–19, 26, 31, 37, 40,
43, 46, 53, 98, 130; color hierarchy in, 102; identification in,
10–11; and identity, 75; miscegenation in, 94; and morality,
40–41; mulatto in, 4, 7, 17, 153;
and nationalism, 7; and race, 7;
race snobbishness of, 15; and
racialism, 3; racism in, 94; reader
of, 10–11, 14; and sentimental
fiction, 9; sexual stereotypes in,
9; violence against, 97; in Wilson, 122, 126; and women,
171n14. *See also* reform
aesthetics: in Child, 44, 56–57,
58; in Hildreth, 100; and race,
44, 57; in Stowe, 110, 116;
white standards of, 74; in Wilson, 133
African Americanist criticism,
9–10
agency: in Brown, 83; of mulatta,
10; in Stowe, 112, 114, 117,
173nn55, 58; in Wilson, 138,
145
allegory, 23, 120, 142, 144,
177n60

amalgamation, 4, 159n6. *See also*
miscegenation
American Anti-Slavery Society,
40, 41, 53
American Colonization Society,
77
Andrews, Tina, 148–149, 152, 154
Andrews, William L., 43, 73; "The
Novelization of Voice in Early
African American Narrative,"
69
androgyny, 139
Anglo-Saxonism, 28, 29, 38, 61,
71, 74, 76. *See also* whites
Anthony, Susan B., 83
assimilation: in Brown, 11; in
Child, 19, 36, 47, 48, 49; in
Wilson, 145
audience. *See* reader
authenticity, 9–10, 69, 81
authority: in black writers, 69; in
Brown, 71, 80; in Hildreth,
101; willing submission to,
154
autobiography, ex-slave, 69, 70

Baym, Nina, *Woman's Fiction,* 8
Beaumont, Gustave de, *Marie; or,
Slavery in the United States,* 97

About the Author

Eve Allegra Raimon is an associate professor of arts and humanities at the University of Southern Maine, Lewiston-Auburn College. Among her publications are articles on the political history of miscegenation and the interdisciplinary teaching of race. She is presently editing a collection of essays about Harriet Wilson's *Our Nig*.